When Women Walk with God

Dedicated to

_____

From

_____

He has shown you, O mortal, what is good.
And what does the Lord require of you? To act justly and to
love mercy and to walk humbly with your God.

Micah 6:8 (NLT)

When Women Walk With God
100 Day Devotional

Published by: Huba Publishing
Cover Design and Text Design: Huba Publishing.
Images used under license from Canva.com
Prepared for printing by Huba Publishing, Johannesburg, South Africa

ISBN: 9780620758680

Contents

Reviews

"The message encoded in these devotions permeated my spirit and opened insight on things that I undermined, and I began to pay attention to them. These devotions became a daily dose that sustained me and took to another level spiritually."
- Ps Zodwa Dlamini

"As a man, I was inquisitive and just opened it randomly at any place and got hooked. The devotional pieces are uplifting and inspirational."
 - Gideon Kok

"The book is very inspirational and very spiritual. It reminded me of my purpose in life as a Christian and a praying woman. I was reminded about the importance of prayer and connecting with my God."
 - Lesego Malebo

"I find myself going back to these devotionals and have made it part of my evening prayer."
- Eileen van Wyk

Dedications

I write this devotional, in memory of my Grandmother Matseleng "Mmepallo" Lydia Masoabi, a woman of God, a worshipper, a woman of meekness! A mother, grandmother, and sister who will forever be missed. A woman after Gods heart. She epitomised the loving nature of mother, who served her community and congregations.

I dedicate this devotional to a true worshipper and warrior for Christ, to my Mother Seabi Esther Tlhomelang. To my father Ramoreo Daniel Tlhomelang, a faithful servant of God. Thank you for the spiritual leadership in my life and for always showing us that God is first, the author and finisher of our lives.

My brothers, Obakeng John Marcus one pure soul, and an embodiment of what the full creation of the being is. He reminds me always we are all mind, body, and spirit and all these need to be in alignment. To Tshiamo Kenneth Goodenough, my lil' bro, thank you for the spirit in you that affirms that we are all good enough and that the measure of our being is from the Lord Almighty. Finally to my husband Cuan Matthew Prince, for walking beside me and being a witness of my Christian walk.

This is for all women! God is always with us and will never leave us. He has given us life, and we should live it more abundantly!

Introduction

Imagine what it was like for Adam and Eve to walk in the Garden of Eden and talk to God. Just imagine the daily conversations they would have. The calmness of spirit, knowing that you're with your Big Daddy and at any moment, in a split second you call on him, and he is with you.

This environment has never changed. It is only we who choose not to have that conversation. We distance our lives from the one who created us, and we select the barriers ourselves. God is always yearning to commune with us, especially us women. He formed us in from Adam's rib, and he named us Eve, the mother of all the living. We have been given a responsibility to take care of this world, to form and shape God's creations as they pass through us and get nurtured by us. We are to walk with God as he has ordained us to be co-creators with him.

Walking with God is an essential part of Christian living, and I hope that these devotionals guide and aid you in your walk with God. I hope it reminds you that you do not walk alone. He has left us with the Holy Spirit to guide us in our journey. We have the power of prayer to connect with him. He left us his Word to nourish and encourage daily so that we can sow into the lives of our families, our children our spouses our friends and our communities, and demonstrate his calling in our lives.

TJ Prince

WALK WITH PURPOSE

"When you walk with purpose, you
collide with destiny."
Bertice Berry

"The longer we carry what is not ours to carry, the deeper the effect is has on us."

TJ Prince

Day 1

All Things Begin with Him

"Therefore if any man be in Christ, he is a new creature: old things are passed away; behold all things are become new."
-2 Corinthians 5:17(KJV)

Start with a spring in your step today. Possess the anticipation that God will turn all your dreams and goals into reality. Remember to do your bit. Do the work, and God will do the rest!

He is the beginning and the end. As you begin this walk, keep Him in mind. When you make your plans, make Him top of your list so that you can walk and talk with him in and throughout this year.

He has already planned ahead of you. Surrender and be obedient. Discover your identity as you walk with Christ. May you reach your destination.

Today's Walk with God

Heavenly Father, please make me the woman you intended me to be so that I may glorify you in everything I do, think and say. *Amen*

Day 2

~

Change & Renew the Mind

"Do not conform to the pattern of this world, but be transformed by the renewing of your mind. Then you will be able to test and approve what God's will is—his good, pleasing and perfect will."
-Romans 12:2 (NIV)

The mind is a powerful thing. Psychologists tell us that our life patterns (our personalities & behaviours) are established when we reach ten years old, and these remain with us for the rest of our lives and cannot be changed.

However, what a great God we have! He tells us clearly that we can change the patterns of our lives, our minds, and our personalities.

This only possible if we focus our thoughts daily on God and allow him to take center stage in our minds and our inner being. We need to renew our minds.

Only then will the transformation will begin. A new creation will be born again in Jesus Christ. "As a man thinketh, so is He."

Today's Walk with God

Let my thoughts be your thoughts. Lord, help me to break the old patterns of my life and be renewed according to your image. *Amen*

Day 3

How Deep the Father's Love for Us

*"How precious is your unfailing love, O God!" - **Psalm 36:7 (NLT)***

I cannot express how much God loves you, but one song does. It is a song by *Inheritance (Live) featuring Graham Cooke*, it says it all in the first verse; "The Lord says, there is nothing you can do to make Him love you more. There is also nothing you can do that would make Him love you less.

He loves you because He loves you because
He loves you because He loves you because
He loves you because He loves you because
He loves you because He loves you because
He loves you because He loves you because

That is who He is. It is His nature to love. You will always be His beloved. His love is unchanging. He loves you 100%.

Look at your life today and see the miracle of his love in your life. One cannot deny his love for us. He paid the ultimate price by giving up his only son just because he loves us 100%.

Today's Walk with God

Lord Jesus Christ, I open my heart to you, I give you 100% of me to you. I believe you love me, because your love is unfailing, unconditional, even though the world may have forsaken me, your love is my strength. *Amen*

Day 4

The Widow of Nain mourning her Son's Death

"Soon afterward, Jesus went to a town called Nain. His disciples went with Him, accompanied by a large crowd. As He approached the town gate, He saw a dead man being carried out, the only son of his mother, and she was a widow. And a sizeable crowd from the town was with her. When the Lord saw her, He had compassion on her and said, "Do not weep." **-Luke 7:11-13 (NIV)**

The story about the Woman of Nain is such a sorrow-filled passage, a mother, a widow following a corpse which held her hopes and dreams. She was walking down to the city gate to bury not only her son but whatever she had left of her own life. In her death row walk, there was a crowd following her. There will always be a crowd, you see. She didn't know that coming up to meet her was the life-giver, also coming with a crowd and they would intersect, life and death would face off. And guess who won? It was the one who conquered death, Jesus Christ, the one who saw her and said to her do not weep as in the same way he said to his mother Mary when he was on the cross. He knew about the resurrection of life and the joy that would bring. That is why he said to her, "Do not weep, he is not dead!" You will have an encounter with Jesus Christ at the city gates when you are just about to check out on life. He is the one who will bring you back to life and bring you joy. Wipe your tears today, because your breakthrough has just arrived! Rejoice and be glad in him.

Today's Walk with God

God forces no one, for love cannot compel, and God's service therefore, is a thing of perfect freedom. - *Hans Denk*

Day 5

~

The First Shall Become Last

*"For even the Son of Man did not come to be served, but to serve, and to give his life as a ransom for many." - **Mark 10:45 (NIV)***

In today's world, where gender roles are changing and have become blurred, this has caused considerable debate, particularly for women in the world. Their role in the kitchen has become obsolete. Women are tackling new fields of work. More and more, they are in positions of leadership and authority.

What does the Bible have to teach us about leadership and servanthood? Jesus Christ was clear in that if you want to lead, you must serve; you must be at the back of the line. We have allowed the belief that for one to lead; one has to be in the front, on top. Authentic leadership is in the humble service to those that you lead. I believe women have learned and honed this valuable skill over the years. They can teach the world the true principles of leadership.

We have the opportunity now to show what authentic servant leadership is. Women! Never underestimate your value or worth or your leadership gift. It is in all of us. Take heed of the example that Jesus Christ set before us, and serve this world that is need of comforters, caregivers, and pathfinders. Be the light of the world.

Today's Walk with God

Heavenly Father, I pray that you give me a spirit of servanthood that I make a difference in my community and to those around me. Guide me, so that I may be a shining example to others. *Amen*

Day 6

Discover Your Purpose: The Woman with the Alabaster Jar

"I tell you the truth, wherever this gospel is preached throughout the world, what she has done will also be told in memory of her."
-Matthew 26:13 (NIV)

Our Lord Jesus Christ is facing his fate, the ultimate sacrifice. They were plotting to arrest and kill him. While he was in Bethany, a woman came with an alabaster jar filled with expensive perfume and poured it over his head and body. The disciples were angered about this act, but he rebuked them.

He revealed to them that this woman is to be honoured and admired. It is as if He knew she was preparing his body for his burial. She was anointing him.

What then is your role in the Christian walk? Find your place. Define your act of faith, no matter how big or small. We are all created for a purpose, find yours. Be like the woman with the alabaster jar. You too will be remembered throughout the whole world.

Today's Walk with God

Almighty Father, let me remember that you created me with a purpose and on purpose, just like the woman with the alabaster jar. May your will be revealed in my life. *Amen*

Day 7

You are Holy & Blameless in His Sight

"Blessed be the God and Father of our Lord Jesus Christ, who has blessed us with every spiritual blessing in the heavens, in Christ. For he chose us in Him before the foundation of the world to be Holy and blameless in his sight."
-Ephesians 1:3-4 (ESV)

God has a way of wiping a slate clean, giving us a new beginning. Doesn't that make you feel distinct? As if something has lifted off your shoulders! You can now breathe.

Being blameless in his sight is just like being drenched in his holiness, entirely from head to toe. Like being caught in the rain. You get completely soaked. When God comes into our lives and fills us, we are drenched and soaked in him. In the scripture above the word says, He chose us in Him to be holy and blameless.

Today's Walk with God

Father, I am holy and blameless in your sight. Thank you for this blessing in my life, may I learn to see it for myself. *Amen*

Day 8

~

The Heart of a Woman is the Wellspring of Life

"Above all else, guard your heart, for it is the wellspring of life."
-Proverbs 4:23 (NIV)

This scripture is often discussed when dealing with matters of the heart, warning women not to give away their hearts so easily to men, especially the wrong type of man. Let us look at it a little deeper and focus on the words, "The wellspring of life." It is the primary purpose of why we should guard our hearts. Women are nurturers and builders of nations. We breathe life and death into our communities, our children, our partners, and we are the guardians of life itself. We have been given an enormous responsibility, therefore guard it & focus on the Lord. Scientists have realised that the heart actually controls the brain. As we know, one can be brain dead, and yet the body can continue to function. But once a person's heart stops, all life stops. We need to be mindful of this. The definition of the word *'wellspring'* is an old English word which means, an abundant source, a good source of something, or something that is inexhaustible, one that is never-ending and good. We are cautioned to guard this heart, as it holds something valuable, the source of life, both in the physical and in the spiritual. Matthew 12:34 warns us, *"You brood of vipers, how can you who are evil say anything good? For out of the overflow of the heart, the mouth speaks."* Have you checked your heart lately? What are the things that are coming out of your heart? What have you allowed to influence your heart? Watch out for the jealousy, envy, and discontent of the heart. Continually examine your heart, it is the source of all that is good, joyful and peaceful.

Today's Walk with God

Dear God, search my heart, so that it may reflect your image every day. *Amen*

Day 9

The Woman at the Well. Where can I get this Living Water?

"Jesus answered, "Everyone who drinks this water will be thirsty again, but whoever drinks the water I give them will never thirst. Indeed, the water I give them will become in them a spring of water welling up to eternal life." -John 4: 13-15 (NIV)

The story of the Samaritan woman is one with many interpretations and investigation, but for me, it is a story of each Christian, it is how Jesus meets you where you are, in your situation and your circumstances. You do not have to look far, some of us seek and seek and seek, but fail to see that Jesus is already there to give you what you thirst for, you just have to recognize him. It took a while for the Samaritan to realize that she was indeed speaking to the Saviour. Jesus had to reveal himself to her by prophesying about her life; only then did it dawn on her about the unique experience she was a part of.

She could not wait to tell the whole town about her encounter. Many were saved because of this. You will never be the same when you encounter Christ, it's undeniable! Never look down on your situation, it may be the situation where you are to meet with Christ one-on-one! Imagine that! Just imagine! If you were the women at the well, drinking from his cup and telling the world about his Glory and Majesty!

Today's Walk with God

Lord Jesus, we often live empty lives, like empty vessels. Take this opportunity to fill my soul that it overflows with living water that forever breaks the drought in my life. *Amen*

Day 10

~

Who is Your Naomi?

Ruth 1-4 (NIV)

The former first lady Michelle Obama was doing her farewell speeches as she moved out of the White House. She implored and challenged women around the world to mentor each other in their success.

She has been a role model for women across the world. She clothed herself with dignity and pride, elegance, and maturity. She exuded her feminine self without any shame, and she walks away from that office, with her head held high. An inspirational woman!

How many of us can say we too have had exemplary women in our lives? Ruth had Naomi. This relationship has been debated for years. There has been commentary depicting Naomi as a very subservient woman who lived in a patriarchal system. A woman who learned to survive in that system.

Nevertheless, let us examine the character of Naomi further. She is a noblewoman, a woman who had lost everything, a husband, and her two sons. This diminished her value in her community. She was left with two widowed daughters-in-law. What value were they going to add to her life?
With no other option, she ordered them to go back to their father's house, but Ruth was not persuaded. She refused to go because of the love she had for Naomi (this is rare... mothers-in-law are usually the enemy in today's society)

Naomi decided to take on another woman's daughter and make her, her own. She counselled her, advised her, and put plans in place for Ruth to be successful in her life.

Ruth got married and bore a son, her value and self-dignity were restored, because Naomi was willing to mentor another woman.

Who is your Naomi? Have you found a woman in your life who will counsel you, help you create your path; stand by you when all is lost, a woman who will celebrate in your joy. Take time this year to find your Naomi.

Today's Walk with God

Dear Heavenly Father, thank you for the mentors who light the way when our paths seem most dark. Thank you for buffering our weakness and inadequacies with women like Naomi, who have been there and had the wisdom to motivate us. As we progress in our purpose, I pray that you allow us to tune our ears towards enlightenment and lead others out of the darkness, into the light. In Jesus name, we pray. *Amen.*

My Prayer of Purpose

WALK
IN
FAITH

Faith is taking the first step even when
you don't see the whole staircase.
Martin Luther King Jnr

"A woman of faith is protected by God, strengthened by God, and victorious in God, because she has favour. And that woman is You"

Unknown

Day 11

Be Led by the Holy Spirit

"As many as are led by the Spirit of God, these are the sons of God."
- Romans 8: 14 (NIV)

The leadership of the Holy Spirit is what validates our sonship in Christ. The Holy Spirit is our seal of promise about the coming of the Lord. Without the Holy Spirit, our comforter, counsellor, advocate, helper, strength provider, and intercessor, we cannot successfully run our Christian race.

Jesus had to leave, so the Holy Spirit could come and dwell in and amongst us. Being led by the Holy Spirit is non-negotiable in our lives.

We need Him to lead us more than the air we breathe. On the day of Pentecost the Holy Spirit came down like a whirlwind and descended on the Apostles and all those who were in the upper room. From that day onwards, they all became changed men. They received the power of God from on high and began to change the world. Without the Holy Spirit and His leadership, we are not able to be everything that God has called us to be.

Today's Walk with God

A woman of faith is protected by God, strengthened by God, and victorious in God, because she has favour!
And that woman is you! *Amen.*

Day 12

~

My God is Faithful & So Am I

"For the LORD is good and his love endures forever; his faithfulness continues through all generations."
-Psalm 100:5 (NIV)

Faithfulness is defined as loyalty, trustworthiness, or steadfastness. It is characteristic of a person who is reliable and who is faithful to God, His Will, and His Word. It means being faithful is not only in deeds but also in word.

Isn't that a challenge! God's faithfulness never changes in our lives! We need to build God's faithfulness to be part of our character. It is going to require that we become obedient, we keep our word, we follow through, we are not doubtful, we do what we say! It is very close to integrity, a challenging virtue for most of us, but if we struggle in this area, God says in his word, that we must choose to be faithful in all things. Be trustworthy in everything *-1 Timothy 3:11*.

You don't have to do it in your strength, pray, and do everything through him who gives you power.

Today's Walk with God

Faith is central to the prayer life and activism of Mothers' Union. It demonstrates God's love in action. It adds a spiritual dimension to a local community activity. It develops concern for issues worldwide. - *Mothers Union member*

Day 13

Faith & Humility of the Canaanite Woman

"Yes, it is, Lord,' she said. 'Even the dogs eat the crumbs that fall from their master's table.' Then Jesus said to her, 'Woman, you have great faith! Your request is granted.' And her daughter was healed at that moment."
- Matthew 15: 27-28 (NIV)

In the passage, Jesus had retreated to the region of Tyre and Sidon. On the way, he was met by a woman who came crying to him to save her daughter. As she begged and pleaded, Jesus did not say a word to her. Imagine, in all your agony and shame and humility, pleading and asking for help. He says nothing.

From the previous verses, we learn that he had been travelling, healing, and performing miracles; he had been chased out by the opposition and had to deal with conflict. He was tired, so he withdrew to Tyre and Sidon. Just as he was about to rest, this woman shows up. She was a Canaanite, a Gentile from a nation which was an enemy to Israel. She didn't deserve the miracle; moreover, she was bothering Jesus, so the disciples decided to chase her off. She knew that the word of the Lord does not return empty! She did not give up but believed that at that moment, her miracle was about to happen.

It didn't matter what tribe she came from; she was going to get what she came to get, even if it is just crumbs. It was her relentless faith that got Jesus to speak and granted her, her miracle. How are you going to get Jesus to speak?

Today's Walk with God

The closer you remain to Jesus, the easier it will be for you to grow spiritually. *Amen*

Day 14

~

Have Faith like a Mustard Seed & Move Mountains!

"He replied, "Because you have so little faith. Truly I tell you, if you have faith as small as a mustard seed, you can say to this mountain, 'Move from here to there,' and it will move. Nothing will be impossible for you."- Matthew 17:20-21 (NIV)

Believing in possibilities when all things seem to be falling apart is a test of faith! Finding the silver lining is the blind belief that something is about to change. The disciples could not understand why they couldn't drive out the demon out of the boy. The father of the boy had given up hope and was disappointed with the disciples' failure to help him. He then went to Jesus directly.

It is interesting here that Jesus was quite upset with both the father and his disciples. He challenged them about their faith, how little faith they had, in seeing the boy healed. They now had to rely on Jesus to heal the boy!

The lesson here is that you and I have to believe in ourselves, with no ounce of doubt that you can and will accomplish anything. Blind faith, for most of us, sounds ridiculous! When all facts, science, and logic tells us that a situation is not going to change!

Jesus reprimands us by instructing us to have faith as small as a mustard seed, and with that, you can move mountains! He further qualifies his statement by saying, this only happens through prayer and fasting. It illustrates to me that faith without works is dead. You have to do more than just believe. Faith is therefore the driving belief to see something come to pass. Have faith today, look out for what is causing you to doubt.

Today's Walk with God

Never lose an opportunity of urging a practical beginning, however small, for it is wonderful how often is such matters the mustard-seed germinates and roots itself.

Florence Nightingale

Day 15

~

The Crippled Woman in the Synagogue

"On a Sabbath Jesus was teaching in one of the synagogues, and a woman was there who had been crippled by a spirit for eighteen years. She was bent over and could not straighten up at all. When Jesus saw her, he called her forward and said to her, "Woman, you are set free from your infirmity." Then he put his hands on her, and immediately she straightened up and praised God."
-Luke 10:13-17 (NIV)

Sometimes we become so comfortable in our pain and surrender to our situation, never thinking that God can see us. Let me remind you; you are not anonymous, stop playing small.

God sees you in your naked self. He knows the places in our lives that need to be healed and to be straightened up. He's the only one who can go to those places you hide so well. God sees you!

Today's Walk with God

Lord Jesus, come into the dark places of my life and shine light upon them, so I may straighten up too, and receive your grace.
Amen

Day 16

Woman! Be Relentless, Reach out and Touch

"For she said to herself, "If I may touch the hem of His garment, I shall be made well. But Jesus turned around, and when he saw her He said, "Be of good cheer daughter, your faith has made you well."
-Matthew 9: 21-22 (NIV)

This dear daughter of God had suffered for twelve years. She had been bleeding, and her life was slowly seeping away. She must have suffered many things as a result of her ailment. She could have been smelling and weak from the constant flow. One day, she told herself that if she reached out and touched the Master's garment, her years of pain and agony will end.

Her faith, not her friend's faith, made her well. It does not matter how long the pain has lasted for. A woman once told me that you need to keep on praying until you leave an imprint of your knees on the carpet!

You have to be relentless! Make up your mind and reach out to Jesus for yourself in faith. See how that long-standing faith will turn things around forever.

Today's Walk with God

When you are standing in the middle of a storm, you have two choices: Pray to God that it goes away. Or, start praying to God that he gives you the wisdom to figure out why you're standing in the middle of a storm. - *Shannon L. Alder*

Day 17

~

Woman, Go and sin no more!

"Brothers and sisters, if someone is caught in a sin, you who live by the Spirit should restore that person gently. But watch yourselves, or you also may be tempted. Carry each other's burdens, and in this way, you will fulfil the law of Christ." - **Galatians 6:1-2 (NIV)**

Our Lord Jesus Christ died on the cross for our sins, and by grace, we were forgiven and entered into the Kingdom of God. We received this salvation by doing absolutely nothing! The only request was to accept Jesus as your Lord your God. The story of the adulterous women is one that shows Jesus's promise in action. He said that he would not condemn us for our sins and we will not die, but have eternal life. The woman who was caught in sin was facing death by stoning, yet she escaped the sentence of death and received new life in Christ.

It begs the question, who are we then to condemn others of sin and to persecute them? Who are we to judge? We need to be more supportive of each other's spiritual growth, and in our individual walks with Christ. God gave the woman salvation and then said to her, go and sin no more!

Today's Walk with God

Teach us, good Lord,
to serve you as you deserve;
to give and not to count the cost;
to fight and not to heed the wounds;
to toil and not to seek for rest;
to labour and not to ask for any reward,
save that of knowing that we do your will.
- St Ignatius Loyola, 1491-1556

Day 18

God's Dare

"The Lord again spoke to Ahaz: "Ask for a confirming sign from the Lord your God. You can even ask for something miraculous." But Ahaz responded, "I don't want to ask; I don't want to put the Lord to a test." So, Isaiah replied, "Pay attention, family of David. Do you consider it too insignificant to try the patience of men? Is that why you are also trying the patience of my God? For this reason, the sovereign master himself will give you a confirming sign."
-Isaiah. 7:10-15 (NET)

As we pray in our daily lives, we ask for things, we plead to God for answers, but at the back of our minds, we have a predetermined answer & solution. We make assumptions of God's response – yea of little faith!

Very often, we are surprised by the answer and direction that God gives us and are challenged to be obedient to his word.
I dare you today, to ask God for your heart's desire and be willing to accept the response you get.

Today's Walk with God

She did not wonder how she made it. She already knew the answer. Only with God's help, she powered through. For without his strength, she could do nothing. She looked back and marvelled how far she had come. *Amen*

Day 19

The Power of Your Words!

"So Jesus answered and said to them, "Have faith in God. For assuredly, I say to you, whoever says to this mountain, 'Be removed and be cast into the sea,' and does not doubt in his heart, but believes that those things he says will be done, he will have whatever he says. Therefore I say to you, whatever things you ask when you pray, believe that you receive them, and you will have them." -Mark 11: 22-24

When a mother loses her child, it is a pain I will never comprehend. You question the very existence of God. I found myself in a prayer meeting, where we were comforting a woman who has just lost her child. As we were praying, God challenged our faith. He asked us, "If I say and have proclaimed the things I have said in the word, do you believe them? What is it that you hope for? What are your predictions? A prediction is what someone thinks will happen. A prediction is a forecast. Pre-means "before" and "*diction*" has to do with talking. Therefore, a prediction is a statement about the future. It's a guess, sometimes based on facts or evidence, but not always." What stands out is the word diction; it has to do with talking, what we confess with our tongue! When we were praying, do we honestly believe in what we were hoping for?

Today's Walk with God

In whatever situation, I find myself in Lord, help me to think about the words I speak and the meditations of my hearts that they are in alignment with your word God, may we see his glory! *Amen.*

Day 20

≈

Fear Not. Just do it, I've got your back!

"The LORD is my light and my salvation; whom shall I fear? The LORD is the stronghold of my life; of whom shall I be afraid?"
-Psalm 27:1 (ESV)

Whom shall I fear? Whom shall I fear? God did not give us a spirit of fear! Fear is the biggest obstacle we all have to conquer. It stops us from doing what we are meant to do with our lives. It prevents us from achieving our dreams, the purpose that God has bestowed on us.

I want to finish the race! Therefore, let us be obedient to the voice of God, when he says to you, "Just do it! I've got your back." Doubt often creeps in when we hear this. Anxiety and worry develops. I know for sure that whatever God wants me to do, it is BIG, and it requires that I rely entirely on him.

Finish your task, run your race, make God your stronghold, cling to his word like your holding on for dear life, Make him the parachute, Trust him, it will open!

Today's Walk with God

Help me Almighty God to fully surrender to your will. Help me not to be afraid and to know that you are always with me. *Amen*

My Prayer of Faith

WALK IN PRAYER

Prayer is an act of love; words are not needed. Even if sickness distracts from thoughts, all that is needed is the will to love.
St Teresa of Avila

"Our service to God and others must always be characterized by an attitude of love."

TJ Prince

Day 21

There is Power in a Woman's Prayer

Then Esther sent this reply to Mordecai: "Go, gather together all the Jews who are in Susa, and fast for me. Do not eat or drink for three days, night or day. I and my attendants will fast as you do. When this is done, I will go to the king, even though it is against the law. And if I perish, I perish." -Esther 4: 15 – 16 (NIV)

Esther did not perish! In fact, she got favour before the King and deliverance for the Jews from their enemies. This beautiful woman did not rely on her beauty, charm, position, or grace to secure salvation for her people. She prayed and fasted!

She called on her own people to pray along with her.
There is power in prayer. A woman who can kneel before God can stand before any man. Prayer changes decrees and laws.

Get into your closet and cry out to God. Prayer changes all things. God still rules in the affairs of men. Go to your Father and get the change done. Remember, decisions are made in the throne room of God.

Today's Walk with God

Lord, help me to cry out in every situation, no matter how difficult it may be. *Amen*

Day 22

$\backsim$

Go to the Mountain Top - An Undistracted Experience

"And when He had sent the multitudes away, He went up on the mountain by Himself to pray. Now when evening came, He was alone there." - **Matthew 14:22 (NKJV)**

In ancient times, Prophets and Clergy often went to the mountaintop to pray, to give an offering or to worship. The Bible gives us numerous examples of this. Jesus often went up to the Mount of Olives with his disciples to pray. The mountaintop is the best place to see the panorama of God's creation, where your voice echoes for a distance as your prayers are transmitted to reach God himself.

At the mountaintop, the air is crisp and clean, your lungs are rejuvenated, and your spirit is renewed. Go up the mountaintop! Carry all our burdens there, they may seem burdensome, but you get to leave them there, you get to cry out and shout out your prayer to God, and release all you want to release. You walk away with the gift of leaving it all at the mountaintop.

Today's Walk with God

Lord Jesus, you prayed at the mountaintop, teach me to find my mountaintop, were I may worship you and freely cry out to you, help me find my place to leave my burdens, so I may come down my mountaintop renewed. *Amen*

Day 23

A Day is a Gift from God

"God called the light "day," and the darkness he called "night." And there was evening, and there was morning--the first day."
-Genesis 1:5 (NIV)

"Do not boast about tomorrow, for you do not know what a day may bring."
-Proverbs 27:1 (NIV)

When God created night and day, He said, "This is good." We also sing praises and say, this is the day that the Lord has made I will rejoice..., but, how many of us take the 24hrs we have been granted for granted. Sometimes a day can seem like a lifetime when there is a death or sorrow. When we are happy a day seems so short, and we often hope that it would never end, especially when we are in love. A lot can happen in a day. Days are valuable and unpredictable, not everything is in our control, yet we've all been given an equal gift, "A day from God."

How are you going to spend it? God wants us to understand the importance of each day. It's the only one you have. Today is the only day you can hold onto. It is at this moment, not tomorrow, but today! Therefore, do not miss the power of today and its opportunity!

Today's Walk with God

Dear Lord, Thank you for this new day, for keeping me safe throughout the night. Please protect my heart and mind today. Help me rise above the negativity, harshness, and division that seem to be taking over our world. Help me to focus my thoughts on the things that are right, pure, and true. Help me to be slow to anger. Give me your wisdom and fill me with your peace. May I show the same grace to others that you have shown to me, in Jesus name, I pray. *Amen*

Day 24

~

God's Promise – I'll Stand Up For You

"No one will be able to stand up against you all the days of your life. As I was with Moses, so I will be with you, I will never leave you nor forsake you."- Joshua 1:5 (NIV)

Woman of God, stand up! Stand up! Arm yourself with the word, prayer, and faith. Go out there with your chin up high, walking tall in your heels, with your hips swaying, with the confidence that God has your back.

Woman! God has you covered. He created you. He is the author of your life, the one who can change your circumstances in an instant. He has lifted you up and put you on center stage for you to declare to the world that he is King and you are his daughter, his Princess. As you walk over your challenges, know that he has already been there before you. You are covered! His promises never fail.

Today's Walk with God

Our service to God and others must always be characterised by an attitude of love. *Amen*

Day 25

$\backsim$

Soak Me in Your Holiness

"Purify the altar, and consecrate it every day for seven days. After that, the altar will be absolutely holy, and whatever touches it will become holy." - Exodus 29:37 (NLT)

God tells the Priest to make atonement (make it clean) for the altar and then consecrate (set it apart) it for a week.
The idea is that the entire altar is seen as soaked in holiness.

God wanted his people to see the place where they are to meet him as an extraordinary and holy place.

In the New Testament and today's living, we don't need to an altar to be built to see God's holiness. He gave us his son Jesus Christ, and when we accept him, we get soaked in his holiness.

I hope today you get to see God in all His holiness and you become soaked in his holiness.

Today's Walk with God

Jesus Christ, I welcome you into my life and pray for you to dwell in my life here onwards. *Amen*

Day 26

~~

She Took a Deep Breath & Let it Go!

"Do not be anxious about anything, but in every situation, by prayer and petition, with thanksgiving, present your requests to God. And the peace of God, which transcends all understanding, will guard your hearts and your minds in Christ Jesus."
- Philippians 4:6-7 (NIV)

"For God hath not given us the spirit of fear; but of power, and of love, and of a sound mind."
- Timothy 1:7 (KJV)

Anxiety disorders have become so rife in our society today, more and more psychologist treat people with anxiety. Anxiety is said to be, worry about future events, and the fear is a reaction to current events. These emotions cause physical symptoms, such as a fast heart rate and shakiness.

Some believe that it not as easy to overcome anxiety. It is clear that the Lord did not give us a spirit of fear. Fear is not from God. He gave us a spirit of power, love, and a sound mind. We need to pray in thanksgiving to God for his peace. Guard your heart and mind. Whenever you are fearful, remember this does not come from God. The Lord cares for you.

Today's Walk with God

"Only give heed to yourself and keep your soul diligently, so that you do not forget the things which your eyes have seen and they do not depart from your heart all the days of your life; but make them known to your sons and your grandsons."
-Deuteronomy 4:9 (NASB)

Day 27

People will Hold You to Your Limitations

*"Now a certain man was there who had an infirmity for thirty-eight years. When Jesus saw him lying there, and knew that he already had been in that condition a long time, He said to him, "Do you want to be made well?" The sick man answered Him, "Sir, I have no man to put me into the pool when the water is stirred up; but while I am coming, another steps down before me." Jesus said to him, "Rise, take up your bed and walk." And immediately the man was made well, took up his bed, and walked." – **John 5: 5-8 (NKJV)***

This story baffles me. How exactly did this man get healed? The Bible does not describe what his "infirmity" was, what the text tells us is that Jesus just told him to get up and go. I have a suspicion that this man was physically well, but not well in spirit and mind. He spent 38 years at that pool, waiting for someone to put him inside the pool so he can be healed. When he sees Jesus, he complains to Christ that people are always going in ahead of him. Could people be so selfish not help him after so many years? Or did they notice that he was not that seriously sick? Couldn't he just roll over into the pool?

Maybe he was a hypochondriac? Hypochondria is said a condition in which a person is excessively worried about having a severe illness with themselves or others. It has been claimed that this debilitating condition is a result of an inaccurate perception of the state of body or mind despite the absence of an actual medical diagnosis.

In all this speculation and questioning, the power of the story about the man Healed at the Pool of Bethesda, is that when he came into contact with Jesus, something inside of him ignited, something in him lit up. He came in contact with his creator; He just got up and walked. He was sick and tired of being sick and tired, and with that one command, his life was renewed.

How many of you have been wallowing like a pig stuck in the mud? Feeling despondent that your blessing will never come and you've waited so long but there's no one to help you. You have relied on people, but they have disappointed you, or they are just busy dealing with their own infirmity.

Have you convinced yourself of your story that you cannot even see other possibilities and solutions? Which story have you been telling yourself for 38 years? You need a new story! It is a broken record. It is time to call on the name of Jesus! He will write you a new one.

Today's Walk with God

Lord, I am tired of my story, write me a new one, I want to be healed too. Come into my body, mind and spirit and create in me a new being. *Amen*

Day 28

Do What the Word Says!

*"Do not merely listen to the word, and so deceive yourselves. Do what it says". - **James 1:22 (NIV)***

Many acronyms have been used to describe the purpose of the Bible. Some say it is the Basic Instructions Before Leaving Earth. Others say it is the Basic Instructions Book for Living on Earth, whichever way you describe it, it is the Word of God.

The Word of God is the same yesterday, today and forever, it is relevant as it was in 2000 BC. Its message is for us to prepare ourselves to meet Christ when He returns. God's Word will give you encouragement and hope as you search for life's most profound meaning.

Both the Old and New Testaments are inspired by God. The Old Testament consists of the first thirty-nine books of the Bible from Genesis to Malachi. It reveals God's plan for His people before Jesus' birth. The New Testament, the last 27 books of the Bible (from Matthew to Revelation), reveals the birth, life, death, and resurrection of Jesus. It uniquely describes God's instructions to His church today. Remember to do what it says!

Today's Walk with God

Father, let your word become alive in me. With your grace help me to consistently apply your word in my life and to do what it says. Let your grace be sufficient. *Amen*

Day 29

~

Wisdom! Oh, Wisdom!

"Get wisdom, get understanding; do not forget my words or turn away from them. Do not forsake wisdom, and she will protect you; love her, and she will watch over you."
- Proverbs 4:5-6 (NIV)

There are caves in South Africa, called the Sterkfontein caves where the first human remains were found dating back to 3 million years ago, and the site is called the "Maropeng - Cradle of Mankind." Robert Broom and John T. Robinson made the discoveries from these caves. After one has explored these caves, at the end of the tour, you are asked to make a wish, and in this wish, you can only choose between "luck" and "wisdom." Which one will you choose? That is the question. How many of us want good luck, like to win the national lottery someday.

We seldom ask for wisdom. There is a difference between knowledge, understanding, and wisdom. *"Wisdom is described as the ability to interpret a thing"* Ecclesiastes 8:1.

The Dictionary says, "It is the ability to use your knowledge and experience to make good decisions and judgments." Why then would you need luck if you can have wisdom, then every decision you make will be from a place of knowledge and of good judgement, not from a place of fear and doubt and false hope.

Today's Walk with God

Lord, teach me wisdom so that she may watch over me! *Amen*

Day 30

The Rewards of Having Opposition

"If you listen carefully to what he says and do all that I say, I will be an enemy to your enemies and will oppose those who oppose you."
-Exodus 23:22 (NIV)

Have you ever noticed the moment you are onto something, something really good? You get hit with opposition from all sides. The nay-sayers come out of the woodwork.

God says, don't worry about the opposition. It is good for you. You are about to birth something great! Your prayer is about to get fulfilled. Your miracle is just around the corner. Don't get dismayed.

Your Blessing is on its way. Remember to thank the opposition, when you get the reward. Amen!

Today's Walk with God

Lord, I am open to whatever you have for me. It may not be what I have planned, but I trust your perfect plan for my life. I know nothing is too hard or too wonderful for you. *Amen*

My Prayer

WALK IN OBEDIENCE

God's promises are all on condition of humble obedience.
Ellen G. White

"Sometimes the answer to our prayers in not gaining but losing, which eventually is the gain."

Anonymous

Day 31

Wait Upon the Lord & Receive Abundant Prosperity!

"For evildoers will be cut off, but those who wait for the LORD, they will inherit the land. Yet a little while and the wicked man will be no more; and you will look carefully for his place and he will not be there. But the humble will inherit the land and will delight themselves in abundant prosperity."
-Psalm 37:9-11 (NIV)

Patience is one virtue most of us struggle with. It is one attribute that needs to be nourished & groomed in our lives. We are not all born with patience. God has an interesting way to teach us this. He gives us a promise, an incentive. He never asks us for something, without understanding the consequences and the rewards thereof.

In this passage, He teaches us that if we are steadfast, diligent, meek, and obedient, we shall inherit the earth, and at the same time, the wicked will not be seen. Our reward will be abundant prosperity.

If you read in the earlier verses in verse 7, God goes further to teach us that we should not fret about those who go about attaining prosperity in their wicked ways, He says we need to stay humble, your turn will come, don't worry about what others are doing, focus on him.

In our world today, we see others gathering riches unethically, in politics, and business at the expense of others. It is disheartening to see how the world has become obsessed with "success" by any means. We need to learn that all things belong to him and to him, it all shall return. We are instruments to be used for his glory and not our own. Remember to be humble and wait upon the Lord. Your turn is just around the corner.

Today's Walk with God

We need to learn that all things belong to him, and to him it all shall return. We are instruments to be used for his glory and not our own. Remember to be humble and wait upon the Lord. Your turn is just around the corner. *Amen.*

Day 32

When you've got Nothing Left. That's when He's at His Best

"Not that we are competent in ourselves to claim anything for ourselves, but our competence comes from God. He has made us competent as ministers of a new covenant—not of the letter but of the Spirit; for the letter kills, but the Spirit gives life."
- ***2 Corinthians 3:5-6 (NIV)***

Isn't it funny and somewhat frustrating that when you are just about to quit, at the bottom of the pit, God is there you pick you up, whatever is left of you?

We often accuse God of not being there, yet he was waiting for you to rely on His strength and not your own. I am weak when you are strong. Next time you have that shrinking feeling. Call on him first.

Today's walk with God

Lord, grant us the simplicity of faith and a generosity of service that gives without counting cost. A life overflowing with Grace poured out from the One who gave everything that we might show the power of love to a broken world and share the truth from a living Word Lord, grant us simplicity of faith And a yearning to share it. - *John Birch*

Day 33

~

Thank You Lord for Closing that Door Shut!

"To the angel of the church in Philadelphia write: These are the words of him who is holy and true, who holds the key of David. What he opens no one can shut, and what he shuts no one can open. -Revelations 3:7 (NIV)

Don't we love the second part of this scripture, 'What he opens no one can shut...' We praise God for opening the doors and the blessing that come with it. There is a song by Michelle Williams that says, *"When Jesus Says Yes, nobody can say no!"* it echoes the scripture above. However, wait, how come we never thank and praise the Lord for keeping some door shut! Let's delve into the second part of this scripture, 'what he shuts no one can open.' God has sometimes closed doors on you for your protection, other times to direct you in a specific path. I once applied for promotion in my organisation and knew that I was the best candidate to fulfil the role, but I was not successful. I spent a week moping about it and then just realised that was not the path for me. He had something better in place for me; all I had to be was to be patient & obedient. John 3:30, reminds us, *"He must become greater; I must become less."* There isn't much teaching about how to deal with closed doors. Most people often spiral into depression, anger, and finally give up, forgetting to ask God why he shut the door. We self-loathe and find a reason for our misfortunes or even blame God himself.

Today's Walk with God

Dear God, It's me standing in the need of prayer. Help me to recognise you in the areas where you have shut the door. *Amen*

Day 34

Whom Shall I Fear?

"The LORD is my light and my salvation-- whom shall I fear? The LORD is the stronghold of my life-- of whom shall I be afraid?"
-Psalm 27:1 (NIV)

How often do you rely on your strength? Isn't that showing little faith in Christ and his power to transform our lives?

God will lift up your head above your enemies; they shall stumble and fall because you have made him Lord of your life. Jesus Christ keeps his promises, he will hide you under his shelter in days of trouble, and he will conceal you in the shadow of this tent.

Petition the Lord to teach you his ways and to lead you into a path that leads you to him.

Today's Walk with God

God, help me to cherish the last time I used my hands
to touch someone with love,
to hold someone with comfort,
to reach out to someone with compassion
to make something constructive
to place power into another's hands
So that I may always touch, hold, reach out, make and place;
and let my hands lead me
in a life of action
where my words may follow. *Amen*
Rachel Halsall

Day 35

Position & Power

"Let everyone be subject to the governing authorities, for there is no authority except that which God has established. The authorities that exist have been established by God."
- **Romans 13:1(NIV)**

TD Jakes once said these words in one of his sermons, "Man should not seduce you into positions without the presence of God!" Without the presence of God, the position means nothing.

In the corporate world, we all aspire to go up the corporate ladder in position and power. People do what it takes to be at the top, in a survey conducted by the Center of Creative Leadership, they discovered that one of the sources of power is 'the power of relationships.' It is most often used to promote one's own personal agenda. Another finding was that twenty-eight percent of the leaders surveyed agreed that top leaders misuse power in their organization.

Let's take lessons from King Nebuchadnezzar. The Bible tells us how God dealt with his self-praise and ego in the book of *Daniel 4: 29-34 (NIV)* as follows;

"Twelve months later, as the king was walking on the roof of the royal palace of Babylon, he said, "Is not this the great Babylon I have built as the royal residence, by my mighty power and for the glory of my majesty?" Even as the words were on his lips, a voice came from heaven, "This is what is decreed for you, King Nebuchadnezzar: Your royal authority has been taken from you. You will be driven away from people and will live with the wild animals; you will eat grass like the ox. Seven times will pass by for you until you acknowledge that the Most High is sovereign over all

kingdoms on earth and gives them to anyone he wishes."
Immediately what had been said about Nebuchadnezzar was
fulfilled. He was driven away from people and ate grass like
the ox. His body was drenched with the dew of heaven until
his hair grew like the feathers of an eagle and his nails like the
claws of a bird. At the end of that time, I, Nebuchadnezzar,
raised my eyes toward heaven, and my sanity was restored.
Then I praised the Most High; I honoured and glorified him
who lives forever."

Today's Walk with God

In your leadership journey, remember that all power and
position come from alone. *Amen*

Day 36

True Fasting, What is it?

Every Wednesday, I meet with other young women at church. We call ourselves Pro 31 Cell group. It was my turn to lead the prayer group and decide to choose the topic, True Fasting.

The period of Lent is the 40 days of fasting and the spiritual preparation to Good Friday. It's a time when Christians need to get back to the basics of our beliefs and practices which one of them is fasting. This act of worship is always reserved for Lent and it is still a topic of debate among believers.

We decided to go through scriptures to understand the practice of fasting; I encourage you to read these scriptures when you prepare for Lent.

1. Why & when should we be fasting? - *Luke 5:33-35*
2. How then should we fast? - *Matthew 6: 16-18*
3. What is your intention for you fasting? *Isaiah 58:1-7*
4. The faithfulness of fasting - *Ezra 21-23 & 31*

Today's Walk with God

Lord, teach us to understand your word and your will as we prepare ourselves to get closer to you. As we fast in remembrance of the forty days, Jesus Christ spent in the desert resisting the temptations of Satan, help us remember that we too are dust, and to dust, we shall return, but in your resurrection, we too shall see your Glory. *Amen*

Day 37

Letting Go and Letting God!

"God is our refuge and strength, an ever-present help in trouble. Therefore, we will not fear, though the earth gives way and the mountains fall into the heart of the sea, though its waters roar and foam and the mountains quake with their surging."
- Psalm 46:1-3 (NIV)

We are often tempted to take matters into our own hands, to think that we are in control and that our plans are always right! Oh, the arrogance and pride we have! Remembering Ash Wednesday, it reminds us that we are mortal beings, dust you are, and to dust you shall return. As humans, we have this need to control and manage our lives without discernment and guidance of the Holy Spirit.

I challenge you to allow God to work in your spirit to take control and rule over your life. You will need to surrender all you have to him and trust him. Trust him like the Psalm says, "God is indeed our refuge and strength and ever-present in our troubles." Let him in so he may deal with your troubles as the creator and finisher of all things.

Today's Walk with God

The longer we carry what is not ours to carry, the deeper the effect in us. *Amen*

Day 38

~

Forgive us our Trespasses as we forgive those who Trespass Against Us

"You, then, why do you judge your brother or sister? Or why do you treat them with contempt? For we will all stand before God's judgment seat. It is written: "as surely as I live,' says the Lord, 'every knee will bow before me; every tongue will acknowledge God.' " So then, each of us will give an account of ourselves to God. Therefore let us stop passing judgment on one another. Instead, make up your mind not to put any stumbling block or obstacle in the way of a brother or sister."
- Romans 14:10-13 (NIV)

Each of us one day will be called to account to the Lord for the time here on earth. There are times when we have let ourselves fall into the trap of comparing sin with one another.

Not only are we deceiving ourselves, but also when we do this, we run the risk of depriving someone of the gift of knowing Christ's love because we have approached them with contempt instead of love. Let us continue to be light in our everyday lives.

Today's Walk with God

We must develop and maintain the capacity to forgive. He who is devoid of the power to forgive is devoid of the power to love. *- Martin Luther King Jr.*

Day 39

Woman stand on a solid rock, all other ground is shifting sands!

"Anyone who listens to my teaching and follows it is wise, like a person who builds a house on solid rock. Though the rain comes in torrents and the floodwaters rise and the winds beat against that house, it won't collapse because it is built on bedrock. But anyone who hears my teaching and doesn't obey it is foolish, like a person who builds a house on sand. When the rains and floods come and the winds beat against that house, it will collapse with a mighty crash."
-Matthew 7:24-27 (NLT)

What kind of ground are you standing on today? Now look down at your feet, what kind of terrain is it? One woman I believe stood on solid ground was Mary Magdalene, she was always at Jesus' feet, she was there when they crucified him, she was there when he rose again, and she was still there to spread the good news with the other disciples. This woman stood on solid ground even though she was from circumstances that would have shaken her tremendously. Jesus cast out seven demons out of her.

"What weakness Mary may have had, making it easy for demons to enter her, we are not told. This we do know, they met their Master in Jesus Christ who came to destroy the works of the devil." -Luke 8:1-3

Mary Magdalene became one of Jesus devoted disciples. She listened to his teaching, followed, and obeyed them until the end. We do not know what happened to her after the resurrection, yet I see one super strong woman!

Against all cultural norms, moral standards of the day, she stood on solid ground and worshipped our Lord Jesus. She was not going to be deterred. She was going to be determined.

61

Today's Walk with God

You can't build a great building on a weak foundation. You must have a solid foundation if you are going to have a strong superstructure. - *Gordon B. Hinkley*

Day 40

Trust Me with the Small Things

"The master said, 'Well done, my good and faithful servant. You have been faithful in handling this small amount, so now I will give you many more responsibilities. Let's celebrate together!'
-Philippians 25:23 (NLV)

As the saying goes, *"To whom much is given, a great responsibility is required."* What's important is that God wants to see first how you handle the small stuff. Can you take responsibility? Can he trust you with a little?

Ask yourself, how often do you look down on the little that you have? Do you complain and become ungrateful? Don't we always want more?

The 'more' you will receive will be determined by how you manage the little you have.

Today's Walk with God

Lord, change the way I manage what I have so to learn how manage more you will bless me with. *Amen*

My Prayer of Obedience

WALK WITH PRAISE

In happy moments, praise God. In difficult moments, seek God. In quiet moments, worship God. In painful moments, trust God. Every moment, thank God.
Rick Warren

*"We know very well that what we
are doing is nothing more than a
drop in the ocean. But if the drop
were not there, the ocean would be
missing something*

Mother Teresa

Day 41

I Dwell in the Place of Abundance

"The Lord your God will make you abundantly prosperous in all the work of your hand, in the fruit of your womb and in the fruit of your cattle and in the fruit of your ground. For the Lord will again take delight in prospering you, as he took delight in your fathers,"
- Deuteronomy 30:9 (ESV)

Everything I own belongs to God! Everything you own belongs to God. I dwell in the place of abundance. These are some of the affirmations regarding success and prosperity. What are yours? God continuously tells us that we can have life and live in abundance. He takes delight in making you prosper. Therefore why is it that not all of us are prosperous? There are some key lessons to be learned;

1. We need to give generously and generationally, not just for the short term because God himself gives generationally.
2. You have to prosper so that your descendants may be blessed. What are you doing in this area?
3. Obedience opens up the heavens when you tithe; God showers you with what he is holding for you. He was just waiting for you.

Remember though you need to take the time to sow your seed, by acknowledging him in everything you do, allow him to give you the divine direction.

Today's Walk with God

Heavenly Father, you promised us to be prosperous; I declare the work of your hand in my finances, in my family and the courage to be blessed beyond my comprehension. Remove people that may be enabling my poverty. Let my cup runneth over, in Jesus name I pray. *Amen.*

Day 42

God's People Should Be Caught up with Praising him!

Praise the Lord, Psalm 150

Praise God in his sanctuary praise him in his mighty heavens.
Praise him for his acts of power praise him for his surpassing greatness.
Praise him with the sounding of the trumpet,
Praise him with the harp and lyre,
Praise him with timbrel and dancing,
Praise him with the strings and pipe,
Praise him with the clash of cymbals,
Praise him with resounding cymbals.
Let everything that has breath praise the Lord.
Praise the Lord.

Today's Walk with God

We know very well that what we are doing is nothing more than a drop in the ocean.
But if the drop were not there, the ocean would be missing something. - *Mother Teresa*

Day 43

Who Would Imagine a King?

"For unto us a child is born, unto us a son is given: and the government shall be upon his shoulder: and his name shall be called Wonderful, Counsellor, The mighty God, The everlasting Father, The Prince of Peace." - Isaiah 9:6 (KJV)

"Mommies and Daddies always believe that their little angels are special indeed and you could grow up to be anything, but who would imagine a king."- Whitney Houston - Preacher's Wife sound track, 1996.

What a beautiful song! We all have aspirations to be anything we want to be in the world, we dream of the careers we want to pursue and the success we want to have in the world. Mother Mary would have never thought that her only child would be King, The Messiah, The I AM, The only begotten son.

Who would have imagined him as King of all Kings? A meek and humble man who took on flesh and became like us shared in our human-ness, yet he is the ruler of all things. Who would imagine him as King?

They mocked him, spat on him, yet they still gave him a crown, a crown of thorns. They did not know what they were doing? Who would imagine him as King? He was born in a manger, died on a cross, and buried in a borrowed tomb.

Who would imagine Him as King?

His majesty and glory was revealed to us as he conquered death and rose from the dead. He appeared to us, yet still, we did not recognise him. Who would imagine Him as King?

He ascended to heaven back to his Father, where he resumed his position on the throne and left us his spirit to forever be with us. He left us a promise in that we too will be reunited with him and the Father and that His Kingdom will never end. He told us that we are heirs in his Kingdom. Now, who would have imagined that!

All this is true in fulfilment of the Word of God. We do not have to imagine him as King, because He *is CHRIST THE KING* now and forevermore.

Today's Walk with God

Heavenly Father, Our Lord Jesus Christ was born out of a humble beginning; remind us never to forget where we come from, and never to scorn our origins. You know the plans for us to make us prosper. You had weaved our destinies before we were born. I pray that you help us to be steadfast in our walk with you to discover our kingship. *Amen*

Day 44

It is Well with My Soul

"Please run now to meet her and say to her," Is it well with you? Is it well with your husband? Is it well with the child? And she answered it is well." - 2 Kings 4: 26(NASB)

How can this Shunammite woman say it is well in the face of death? In fact, her dead son was a product of a prophetic word given by Prophet Elisha. After years of being wealthy, yet childless, she finally had a son, and then he died! Nevertheless, this woman did not begin to speak any evil about God. She declared three powerful words: *It is well!*

Daughter of God, know this, what you say matters. Your faith is first seen by what you say. This woman went to her source and got her son back. Go back to God and declare that every dead thing in your life will come alive again.

It reminds me of the hymn, "It is well with my soul," written by Horatio Spafford.

Horatio's Story is the same as of the Shunammite Woman: The hymn was written after traumatic events in his life. In 1871, the Great Chicago Fire ruined him financially. He had been a successful lawyer and had invested significantly in the property business. The great fire extensively damaged all his investments.

His businesses were further hit by the economic recession of 1873, at which time he had planned to travel to Europe with his family on the SS Ville du Havre. In a late change of plan, he sent the family ahead of him while he dealt with the business following the Great Chicago Fire.

While crossing the Atlantic, the ship sank rapidly after a collision with a sea vessel, and all four of Spafford's daughters died. His wife Anna survived and sent him the now famous telegram, "Saved alone."

Shortly afterward, as Spafford travelled to meet his grieving wife, he was inspired to write these words as his ship passed near where his daughters had died. "It is well with my soul."

Today's Walk with God

Therefore, speak life, and you shall experience the presence of God. Whatever the situation, your faith, and words must match God's Word. With God, nothing shall be impossible. *Amen*

Day 45

❧

Let us be Like Jesus and Feed the Multitudes!

*"We have here only five loaves of bread and two fish," they answered. "Bring them here to me," he said. And he directed the people to sit down on the grass. Taking the five loaves and the two fish and looking up to heaven, he gave thanks and broke the loaves. Then he gave them to the disciples, and the disciples gave them to the people. -**Matthew 14:17-19 (NIV)***

At Grandma's house, miracles always seem to happen around the dining table. Food seems to multiply and multiply. Like magic! There is always more than enough to eat, made from very little. It is a women's skill to turn a few ingredients into a full meal. Jesus did the same when he fed multitudes with two loaves and fish and fed the multitudes. He preached and shared the good news with them.

We need to do the same not only at our dinner tables but for those living in poverty and hunger. So many families go to bed without food, how then we expect then to hear the word. I encourage you today to make miracles happen. To share with those around you and see how God increase your plate. We are here to serve and not to be served.

Today's walk with God

Not all of us can do great things. But we can do small things with great love. - *Mother Teresa*

Day 46

Ride the Storms of Life with God as your Guide

For many days neither sun nor stars appeared, and the severe storm kept raging; finally, all hope that we would be saved was disappearing. Therefore take courage, men because I believe God, that it will be just the way it was told to me. -Acts 27: 20 & 25 (HCSB)

Storms are part of life. We have to build our lives around for the inevitable storms. In the scripture above, Paul was a prisoner on a ship on a journey to Rome. On the trip, the Centurion and the Captain decided to take a different route. They ignored Paul's advice and ran into a mighty storm, endangering all on board.

They spent days and nights, with no hope in sight, but Paul knew God's plan for their lives, and he was faithful. Don't let the 'no hopers' pull you down. Cut out the faithless people. You sometimes have to remove your Plan B and stay with God's plan A.

All the two hundred and seventy-six on board found safety ashore on an island called Malta and three months later arrived in Rome and Paul continued with his ministry.

Today's Walk with God

With Gods help, help me succeed in riding the storms of my life. You promised that you will help me and never leave me. *Amen*

Day 47

The Affirmation of another
Woman

"As Jesus was saying these things, a woman in the crowd raised her voice and said, "Blessed is the womb that bore You, and blessed are the breasts that nursed You." But He replied, "Blessed rather are those who hear the word of God and obey it."
-Luke 11: 27-28 (BSB)

As Jesus was preaching to the people, a nameless woman was astounded by the wisdom in the lesson that was being taught. From her point of view, Jesus was a gentleman who has been raised well, to be able to say such things. He was respected and had the attention of everyone. Indeed his mother did something right. Her focus was on how he was raised. This woman affirms Mary and the right things she did. As women, what do we say when we see the fruit of our wombs as compared to others? Sometimes our venomous tongues curse wombs of other women. We insult their children born of these wombs. How we praise each other so little?

This Nameless woman's message was far more than just praising Jesus's mother; she was affirming who He was too, a Son of Man, born of Mary, giving him an identity, in a world where sons and daughters never know their parents.

Jesus responds to her differently. He directs her to the one whom we should all be glorifying and affirming, our God! His word is what we need to observe. He is asserting that we are more than just mortals, but sons and daughters of the King.

Today's Walk with God

Lord God, Help me to affirm other women, in private and in public, to let them know that they too are significant and are doing an excellent job in raising future generations of tomorrow. *Amen*

Day 48

He is Mighty to Save!

*"He saved them - to defend the honour of His name and to demonstrate His mighty power." - **Psalm 106:8 (NLT)***

The Lord wants to work with your situation as a demonstration of His mighty power. He wants to intervene and save us just because He is God.

We may fail Him, but He does not intend to abandon us. He will defend the honour of His name and work wonders in your life.

Today's Walk with God

Lord, may your mighty power be demonstrated in my situation so that others will know that you are God and there is no one like you. *Amen*

Day 49

My Redeemer Lives!

*"Therefore if there is any encouragement in Christ, if there is any consolation of love, if there is any fellowship of the spirit, if any affection and compassion, make my joy complete by being of the same mind, maintaining the same love, united in spirit, intent on one purpose."- **Philippians 2:1-2 (ESV)***

I know that my Redeemer lives and at the end, he will stand upon the earth and look upon us who believe and say, "My good and faithful servants, you have shown love and compassion to each other. You filled the world with love your whole life through."

Today's Walk with God

Lord, thank you for fulfilling your promises in my life, thank you for the joy, and the fullness of spirit. Your presence is my life is my anchor. *Amen*

Day 50

I will Rise on Eagle's Wings

*"But they that wait upon the Lord shall renew their strength; they shall mount up with wings as eagles; they shall run, and not be weary; and they shall walk, and not faint." - **Isaiah 40:31 (KJV)***

What does an eagle do when a storm is approaching? It flies high in the sky, and when the wind comes, it is lifted above the storm where it waits for the storm to subside.

The action of the eagle reminds me of a song by Juanita Bynum, "I don't mind waiting," she says in it that it is a privilege and an honour to wait on the Lord, and we have to learn how to wait.

We can overcome the storms in our lives, and whatever situations that may come, remember that the Lord God is with you, be patient he is pulling you through it.

Today's Walk with God

Heavenly Father, I sometime feel in despair and loosing hope, renew the right spirit within me so that I may be patient and know to wait. *Amen.*

My Prayer of Praise

WALK
IN
SERVICE

I stand here before you not as a
prophet, but as a humble servant of
you, the people.
Nelson Mandela

"The greatest of a man's power is the measure of his surrender."

William Booth

Day 51

The Passion of our Lord

1. "Father, forgive them, for they do not know what they do." **-Luke 23:34**

2. "Truly, I say to you, today you will be with me in Paradise." **-Luke 23:43**

3. "Jesus said to his mother: "Woman, this is your son." Then he said to the disciple: "This is your mother." **-John 19:26-27**

4. "My God, my God, why have you forsaken me?" **Matthew 27:46 and Mark 15:34**

5. "I thirst." **-John 19:28**

6. They put a sponge soaked in wine on a sprig of hyssop and put it up to his mouth. When Jesus had received the wine, he said, "It is finished;" and he bowed his head and handed over the spirit. - **John 19:29-30**

7. Jesus cried out in a loud voice, "Father, into your hands I commend my spirit." **-Luke 23:46**

Today's Walk with God

But I do not account my life of any value nor as precious to myself, if only I may finish my course and the ministry that I received from the Lord Jesus, to testify to the gospel of the grace of God. *Acts 20:24 (ESV)*

Day 52

⌇

Value is determined by Sacrifice

"For you know that it was not with perishable things such as silver or gold that you were redeemed from the empty way of life handed down to you from your ancestors, but with the precious blood of Christ, a lamb without blemish or defect." - 1 Peter 1:18-19 (NIV)

What is value? Quick Economics 101 before we look into the text. Economic value is said to be the maximum amount a buyer is willing to pay for an item. The onus is on the consumer to determine the value, not the seller. Now that we have that understanding, God was the ultimate bidder for our sins. He paid the highest price and determined our value by giving up his only son Jesus Christ. Wow! You and I have value and were bought by blood and sacrifice so that we may attain eternal life.

The question is, what are you doing to achieve value in your life? What sacrifices have you made? God gave us the ultimate lesson in economics and successful living. You get rewarded in the proportion of your sacrifice. Look at all the prophets, apostle and disciples, each of them had to make a sacrifice. Look at all successful people in the world, Gandhi, Mandela, Mother Theresa; they too had to make some sacrifice.

In all aspect of our lives, if we want to achieve something more significant than what we have today, we have to make the sacrifice. Something has got to give. Where there is no sacrifice, there is no love. Think about it for a moment. As a parent, you sacrifice your energy, day in and out working so you can provide for your family because you love them. Examine your life today and see in which of your life requires sacrifice?

Moreover, are those areas prosperous? Where am I adding value? You are where you are today as a direct result of your sacrifice.

I want to encourage you to work hard for that which you desire, don't give up because as you work it, God will give you the power, the tolerance, the resilience because he knows the price at the end of your journey.

It is like the story of the Chinese bamboo tree. It takes about five years for you to see any sign of growth above ground and then after this period its shoot up to 25 meters tall in just six weeks. It was a five-year sacrifice. There are no shortcuts. Don't be attracted to success without the sacrifice.

Today's Walk with God

Lord Jesus, you paid the ultimate price for our salvation, you placed the highest value upon our lives, thank you father for your sacrifice. Teach me the patience and wisdom to be a person of value, and to work diligently in everything I do, because my success is your success, in the name of Jesus. *Amen.*

Day 53

Serve Wholeheartedly as if You are Serving the Lord.

"Slaves, obey your earthly masters with respect and fear, and with sincerity of heart, just as you would obey Christ. Obey them not only to win their favour when their eye is on you, but as slaves of Christ, doing the will of God from your heart. Serve wholeheartedly, as if you were serving the Lord, not people, because you know that the Lord will reward each one for whatever good they do, whether they are slave or free." - Ephesians 6:5-8 (NIV)

Most believers would beg to challenge and disregard this passage. It is because world leaders today abuse their power and their people, especially the poor and the vulnerable. The rise of corruption and self-enrichment in the world has made it difficult for anyone to heed this message. The wisdom in it is that we need to serve wholeheartedly in everything that we do to the Glory of God and not of man.

This passage reminds me of the young boy Karl Marx, in a letter to his father in 1835, he wrote; *"If we have chosen the position in life in which we can most of all work for mankind, no burdens can bow us down, because they are sacrifices for the benefit of all; then we shall experience no petty, limited, selfish joy, but our happiness will belong to millions, our deeds will live on quietly but perpetually at work, and over our ashes will be shed the hot tears of noble people."*

Today's Walk with God

I am loved by God. There may be days I struggle.
There may be days I feel week.
But there is never a day that God is not there.
His love helps me go forward. *Amen*

Day 54

Get Moving

"What does it profit, my brethren, if someone says he has faith but does not have works? Can faith save him?"
- James 2:14-26 (NKJV)

If you want your circumstances to change, you have prayed, you have fasted, you have believed, and God has shown you what you need to do. Now it's time to move your feet and take the first leap of faith.

You wonder why most of us think that God doesn't answer our prayers, he's waiting for you to make your move or take a different direction.

We get stuck, like a dog chasing its tail, wondering why we are in the same spot.

Faith requires action, even in science, for every action, there is a reaction. We are more afraid of the reaction than trusting God when we take action. I believe that you are going to do it!

Today's Walk with God

Surely the principles of Christianity lead to action as well as meditation. - *William Wilberforce*

Day 55

Abba Father! You are Always There!

"Your word is a lamp for my feet and a light for my path."
- Psalm 119:105 (GWT)

Heavenly Father, even though I sometimes feel like I'm walking in darkness, I remember my Abba Father who gives me the light at the end of my tunnels, who fills me up with gladness.

Your word is like a never-ending spring of wisdom to water my ever-wandering heart. Keep me near you, so my cup never runs dry. Amen

Today's Walk with God

The greatest of a man's power is the measure of his surrender.
- William Booth

Day 56

Let us Become the Body of Christ

"So Christ himself gave the apostles, the prophets, the evangelists, the pastors and teachers, to equip his people for works of service, so that the body of Christ may be built up until we all reach unity in the faith and in the knowledge of the Son of God and become mature, attaining to the whole measure of the fullness of Christ."
- Ephesians 4:11-13 (NIV)

I picked up a "meme" on social media that says, *'We will never change the world by going to church. We will only change the world by being the church.'* The beginning of the church can be traced back to the church in Antioch, where Saul, who later became Paul started his missionary work, as recorded in Acts 11:25-26 (NIV). From this point forth, they went around preaching the word of God and the salvation that comes in believing in Jesus Christ. We are called to build up the body of Christ, to equip his people for works of service so that we can reach unity in the faith, and the full measure of the fullness of Christ.

This is so important, in Ephesians 2:6-7 it is written, *"For he raised us from the dead along with Christ and seated us with him in the heavenly realms because we are united with Christ Jesus. So God can point to us in all future ages as examples of the incredible wealth of his grace and kindness toward us, as shown in all he has done for us who are united with Christ Jesus."*

Today's Walk with God

Lord God, our task is simple; teach us to be examples of your grace and kindness on earth and with one another. To share the love which passes all understanding? *Amen.*

Day 57

Fighting Temptations

"All this I will give you," he said, "if you will bow down and worship me." Jesus said to him, "Away from me, Satan! For it is written: 'Worship the Lord your God, and serve him only.' Then the devil left him, and angels came and attended him."
- Matthew 4:1-11 (NIV)

Then Jesus was led by the Spirit into the wilderness to be tempted by the devil. After fasting forty days and forty nights, he was hungry. The tempter came to him and said, "If you are the Son of God, tell these stones to become bread."

Jesus answered, "It is written: 'Man shall not live on bread alone, but on every word that comes from the mouth of God." Then the devil took him to the holy city and had him stand on the highest point of the temple. "If you are the Son of God," he said, "throw yourself down. For it is written: "He will command his angels concerning you, and they will lift you up in their hands so that you will not strike your foot against a stone." Jesus answered him, it is also written: "Do not put the Lord your God to the test." Again, the devil took him to a very high mountain and showed him all the kingdoms of the world and their splendour. In our lives, we will be tempted in three ways; materialism, pride, and with the lust of the flesh. We have to pass this test. Jesus Christ called on God, so should you.

Today's Walk with God

Lord Jesus, I ask you to help me to fight my temptations, let, your spirit of relentlessness and faithfulness and knowledge of your word hold me steadfast. I pray for the Holy Spirit to be my guide during this time. *Amen*

Day 58

Our Spiritual Gifts

"I wish that all of you were as I am. But each of you has your own gift from God; one has this gift, another has that."
-1 Corinthians 7:7 (NIV)

Regardless of how big or how small your gift is, you are part of the Body of Christ, and every function is essential and significant!

No gift is better or more important than the other. You may be a prayer warrior, a helper, the organiser, the preacher, the healer, the comforter, the prophet, interpreter of tongues.

No one gift is more important than the other, as Christians all of these are part of the body of Christ, so embrace your gift and fulfil your calling.

Today's Walk with God

Lord God, thank you for the gifts you have bestowed upon each one of us. You have equipped us to use our abilities and skills, help me never to neglect my gift, but teach me to use them for your kingdom. *Amen*

Day 59

Deny Yourself

*"Then he said to them all: "Whoever wants to be my disciple must deny themselves and take up their cross daily and follow me. For whoever wants to save their life will lose it, but whoever loses their life for me will save it. What good is it for someone to gain the whole world, and yet lose or forfeit their very self?" - **Luke 9:23-25 (NIV)***

In a conversation with his disciples, Jesus was leading them to make a commitment, a declaration of their faith by asking them where they stand with him. He pretty much outlines what the deal is.

Jesus says to them, deny thyself. Most of us think, Oh No! I need to become a nun to do that! plus and I'm still enjoying life to deny myself earthly things.

He is teaching us that to follow him, we have to submit, obey, and put God first in ALL we do, and we do that daily. The Lord's Prayer says. "Let your will be done..." In each step we take, allow him to lead. Die to your desires and ask him first.

Jesus, himself was tested to demonstrate this in the Garden of Gethsemane, and there he let God's will to be done.

Today's Walk with God

Jesus found the muddiest parts of my heart and planted flowers. - *The soul doctor*

Day 60

You Are Important

"Who can separate us for the love of Christ? Can affliction or anguish or persecution or famine or nakedness or danger or sword? Nor height, nor depth, nor any other created thing will have the power to separate us from the love of God that is in it! You are valued!"
-Romans 8:35 & 39 (HCSB)

You are valued. It doesn't matter what you've done, you are still valuable. Think of a $100 bill, whether you crumple it, step on it, tear it into two pieces, it is still valuable. It doesn't matter what you've done, you are still valuable.

God has a powerful favourable opinion about you. He knows you by name. We are not servants but heirs in his kingdom. When you realise your value, generosity comes, and blessings come. You are important to Jesus Christ, so become bold in his love.

Today's Walk with God

God's love is unchanging. Lord Jesus, help me to realise my value and the love that you have for me. Help me to understand that nothing can change your opinion about me. The value of persistent prayer is not that He will hear us but that we will finally hear Him. *Amen*

My Prayer of Service

WALK IN LOVE

Love's voice reverberates with forgiveness across the room of our heart
Munia Khan

"Jesus found the muddiest parts of my heart and planted flowers."

The Soul Doctor

Day 61

~

I Love, Because He Loved Me

*"A new commandment I give unto you, that ye love one another; as I have loved you, that ye also love one another." - **John 13:34 (KJV)***

*A new commandment I give unto you, that you love one another as I have loved you. By this shall all men know that you are my disciples, if you have love one for another. Whoever claims to love God yet hates a brother is a liar. For whoever does not love their brother and sister, Whom they have seen, cannot love God, Whom they have not seen. – **1 John 4:20***

This hymn informs us how we as Christians should treat one another, it is how God will recognize us. It is not by the regular church attendance or how we can speak in tongues even how we serve our community, or how we can memorize scripture.

All these being good! He said he would recognize us by how much we love one another!

Today's Walk with God

The highest form of worship is the worship of unselfish Christian service. - *Billy Graham*

Day 62

Let us Move from Darkness into Light

"The person who says that he is in the light but hates his brother is still in the darkness. The person who loves his brother abides in the light, and there is no reason for him to stumble. But the person who hates his brother is in the darkness and lives in the darkness. He does not know where he is going, because the darkness has blinded his eyes." -1 John 2:9-11 (ISV)

How do we remove our blindfolds our *'scotomas?'* And walk in the light? A *scotoma* is a Greek word meaning darkness, and it is used to describe a medical condition where a part of your vision/sight is diminished or lost. God asks us to love one another, and in doing so, we will be able to live in the light.

He gives a practical example of how to deal with our scotomas. He further instructs us in his first and greatest commandments that you shall love your neighbour as you love yourself because he gave his only son to die for our sins so that we may live in the light and have eternal life.

Identify what your blind spots are and seek to live in the light so that your blindness may not obstruct your path.

Today's Walk with God

Father, teach me to hear you and show me how you want me to live and relate with others. *Amen*

Day 63

It's Time for You to take up Your Cross

"The one who plants and the one who waters have one purpose, and they will each be rewarded according to their own labour."
- *1 Corinthians 3:8 (NIV)*

"But each one must examine his own work, and then he will have reason for boasting in regard to himself alone, and not in regard to another. For each one will bear his own load."
- *Galatians 6:4-5 (NASB)*

The Lord Jesus Christ carried our burdens to the cross and left us with a promise of eternal life and a slate wiped clean. Such grace! It is often so easy to cast it all to the Lord and not be obedient to what his direction is for our lives because we still believe we are in control. Sometimes our prayers are of demands to God, yet we fail to hear the answer, especially when it is not the one we want to hear. The Christian walk comes with obedience and humility to his word and discernment of the Holy Spirit. It is our responsibility to get plugged in. God is asking you to take up your cross too and fulfil your promises, your obedience, all that he has shared with you to do. It is not going to be easy. Laying it on the cross was never easy. Jesus did it for us, what is stopping you from playing your part?

Today's Walk with God

Faith in action is love - and love in action is service.
- *Mother Theresa*

Day 64

More of Thee, Less of Me

"This is the word that came to Jeremiah from the Lord: "Go down to the potter's house, and there I will give you my message." So I went down to the potter's house, and I saw him working at the wheel. But the pot he was shaping from the clay was marred in his hands; so the potter formed it into another pot, shaping it as seemed best to him. Then the word of the Lord came to me. He said, "Can I not do with you, Israel, as this potter does?" declares the Lord. "Like clay in the hand of the potter, so are you in my hand, Israel."
- Jeremiah 18:1-6 (NIV)

Dear God, take me, break me and make me into what you want me to be. Give me the strength to accept what you send my way and the vision to perceive my arrogant ways and the vain things that I do.

Make me mindful when I'm concerned more with myself than with you. Uncover before me my weakness and greed. Help me discover how easy it is to selfishly become lost in my pride. In Thy goodness and mercy, look done on this weak, erring one. Tell me that I am forgiven for all I've so wilfully done, teach me to humbly start following the path that the dear Saviour trod. So, I'll find at the end of the life's journey a home in the city of God.
Prayer by Helen Steiner Rice - A collection of Encouragement (Adapted)

Today's Walk with God

Lord, shape my heart to be like yours, take over because my mind is like clay, but thank goodness, God knows how to mould it! *Amen*

Day 65

Let's Have Some C.O.F.F.E.E

*"Let all bitterness and wrath and anger and clamour and slander be put away from you, along with all malice. Be kind to one another, tender-hearted, forgiving each other, just as God in Christ also has forgiven you." - **Ephesians 4: 31-32 (KJV)***

I'm not a coffee lover, but my husband is. He loves it black, no sugar. Yeesh! Now, that is the taste of bitterness in the mouth. How can you drink such a thing? Well, I can stomach a creamy coffee with some sugar. It definitely tastes better. The milk and sugar takes the bitterness away.

'Christ, Offers, Forgiveness, For Everyone, Everywhere' He is the milk and sugar to our bitterness and the Bible challenges us to do away with bitterness. It is only through forgiveness can we do away with bitterness. If we don't, it is like drinking that bitter coffee every day and everywhere. It is not easy to forgive, but with Christ as your redeemer and shepherd, you will be able to overcome.

Today's Walk with God

Dear God, it's me again, take this cup of bitterness away from me. Help to find forgiveness in my heart so I may be able to move on and to find peace. In your name, I pray. *Amen*

Day 66

To Find Love, is to Find God

"If I speak in the tongues of men or of angels, but do not have love, I am only a resounding gong or a clanging cymbal. If I have the gift of prophecy and can fathom all mysteries and all knowledge, and if I have a faith that can move mountains, but do not have love, I am nothing. If I give all I possess to the poor and give over my body to hardship that I may boast, but do not have love, I gain nothing."
- 1 Corinthians 13:1-3 (NIV)

The book of Corinthians says it clearly, "If you have no love, you have nothing." Love leads you to find God. There are different kinds of Love. The ancient Greeks, in their pursuit of wisdom and self-understanding, discovered eight different types of Love that we all humans experience at some point. *Eros* or Erotic Love, *Philia* or Affectionate Love, *Storge* or Familiar Love, *Ludus* or Playful Love, *Mania* or Obsessive Love, *Pragma* or Enduring Love, *Philautia* or Self Love, *Agape* or Selfless Love.

The Love that we all need to seek is *Agape* Love. The same Love God has for his creation. This Love is not self-seeking, not boastful, not proud but a love that knows the divine truth and the belief of the greater good in every one of us. We have become consumed by seeking temporary solutions for an eternal yearning. Corinthians 13 gives us the script of what this *Agape* love looks like. In your daily walk, use it as a measuring stick, because if you can find this Love, you have seen God.

Today's Walk with God

Almighty Father, lover of my soul, I will never let go of your love for me. *Amen*

Day 67

He Holds me by the Palm of His Hand

*"Arise, lift up the lad, and hold him by the hand, for I will make a great nation of him." - **Genesis 21:18 (NIV)***

God loves children and would never let any harm come to them because they are innocent. In society today they often bear the wrath of their parents action. Ishmael was about to die of thirst in the desert because his mother was thrown out by Abraham. He surely didn't know what was going on. God gave him a favour and a blessing. If you have experienced pain in your youth that you did not deserve, God promises to hold us by the hand and make great nations of us. Whatever your thirst is, he will quench it.

Today's Walk with God

May the road rise up to meet you. May the wind be always at your back. May the sun shine warm upon your face; the rains fall soft upon your fields and until we meet again, may God hold you in the palm of His hand. *Amen.* – Irish Blessing

Day 68

Little Girl, I say to You, Get Up!

"Taking the child by the hand, He said to her, "Talitha kum!" (which translated means, "Little girl, I say to you, get up!"
– Mark 5:41(NIV)

Jesus Christ had been performing miracles and healing people and on the run. He had just crossed over the lake where a herd of pigs full of demons had drowned. As he reached the shore, he was called by Jairus to come and heal his 12-year-old daughter.

On route, through the crowds, the woman with the issue of blood touched the hem of his garment, and he felt power leave him. Perhaps at this same moment, this little girl died, life left his body.

Maybe the little girl had heard that Jesus was coming to heal her and in her spirit she sensed the power of Jesus leave him, she then lost her faith and died, she could not wait any longer.

Do you see the link? The women with the issue of blood for 12 years had a fighting spirit and faith. She was poor, low in social status, yet took an opportunity when presented to her, while the little girl, born in privilege, his father could summon Jesus for his help, yet she could not hold long enough for Jesus to finish teaching the Gospel.

My interpretation, looking at the two women's stories, is that Jesus Christ was teaching us about faith, his power, and his love for us. He was showing us that, no matter who you are, He is the Alpha and Omega.

He can awaken you from your sleep. He is saying to you don't ever lose focus and hope, even though there may be delays in your healing, He is coming.

Today's Walk with God

I am not dead, but I am asleep. Awaken me and let me Arise into a new being, teach me unrelenting faith, to face any challenge that may come my way. Anoint me with the spirit of resilience to never give up. *Amen*

Day 69

Create a New Behaviour Amongst Us

"You are being renewed in the spirit of your minds; you put on the new man, the one created according to God's likeness in righteousness and purity of the truth. Since you put away lying, speak the truth, each one to his neighbour because we are member of one another. Be angry and do not sin. Don't let the sun go down on your anger."
-Ephesians 4: 23-26 (HCSB)

God is a relational God. For him to move into your life, you need to come to him in truth. How do you expect him to move on your behalf if you are unable to move for another person?

God did not anoint you for you! However, he anointed you for someone else. A spiritual man will follow God's voice above his physical and emotional needs. The closer you remain to Jesus, the easier it will be for you to grow spiritually. Become more like Jesus and walk with God every day.

Today's Walk with God

Father, teach me to hear you and to show me how you want me to live and relate with others. *Amen.*

Day 70

≈

I Love the Lord, He Heard My Cry

"And she was in bitterness of soul, and prayed to the Lord and wept in anguish." -1 Samuel 1: 10 (NIV)

Hannah was barren and mocked continuously. It was a turbulent time in her life. One day, she rose up and quit crying before men. She went to her Maker, the God who created the heavens and the earth.

She went to Shiloh and did something different this time. She prayed to the Lord and wept. Woman, if you can weep before God, you are unlikely to keep crying before men. God changed Hannah's story from barrenness to becoming the mother of one of the highest judges and prophets of Israel.

When women pray, God hears them, and things begin to happen. Arise Woman and cry out to God. Start praying again from today! The situation will change in the face of prayer. Hannah's story ended with great joy and fruitfulness. Yours too will end in joy and happiness in Jesus name.

Today's Walk with God

Lord, may I not be quiet when I should be crying out to you in Jesus name. *Amen*

My Prayer of Love

WALK IN FELLOWSHIP

The Church is the new creation, it is life and joy, it is the sacramental fellowship in which we share the ultimate purpose of God, made real for us now in our hearing the Word and sharing the Sacrament.
Rowan Williams

"As we walk with God, let the peace of God be your guide, you antenna, your true north, and then you will always be led back to the right path."

TJ Prince

Day 71

Fellowship with Him

"That which was from the beginning, which we have heard, which we have seen with our eyes, which we have looked upon, and our hands have handled, concerning the Word of life—the life was manifested, and we have seen, and bear witness, and declare to you that eternal life which was with the Father and was manifested to us—that which we have seen and heard we declare to you, that you also may have fellowship with us; and truly our fellowship is with the Father and with His Son Jesus Christ." - 1 John 1:1-3 (KJV)

At the Last Supper, Jesus spent time with his disciples for the last time, and when they shared bread and wine, he reminded them that every time they do this, they should do it in his memory! He is teaching us that this is one way he will recognise us, in our conduct with one another in our fellowship with each other. It reminds me of a song," Bind us together, Lord with chords that cannot be broken!"

The presence of the Lord is always amplified when believers are together. In these acts, our bond with God is strengthened. Moreover, our relationship is enhanced as a community of believers. Here the disciples tell us that they have seen and bore witness, and they want to share with us the good news, so we may also share in fellowship with them and the Lord Jesus Christ.

Ask yourself, when last did you fellowship with another person about the word of God. Someone in your life may be hoping that you will invite them to church, to a cell group, a prayer meeting or gathering, be like the disciples and encourage others to be in fellowship with the Lord, so we can all share in the walk of faith.

Today's Walk with God

Lord, I am having difficulty loving and relating to an individual, today I take him to God. I bother you Lord with this person and leave him at the throne. *Amen*

Day 72

The Road to Emmaus

"He walks with me and he talks with me." -Luke 24:13-35 (NIV)

"He lives, He lives, Christ Jesus lives today! He walks with me, and He and he talks with me, along life's narrow way!

This hymn reaffirms the resurrected Christ. He walked with the disciples but they did not recognise him. They eventually had supper with him, and still, they did not recognise him.

Imagine yourself, being there at the cross; witnessing the crucifixion and later, the same man who died in front of your eyes, you could not recognise him.

We witness, yet we do not see! Our eyes have seen and heard about the Resurrection of Christ, yet we still we do not see, he walked with us and talked with us, and we do not see?

When will our eyes open? When will we know and recognise him in our lives? When will we invite him to sit with us at the dinner table and acknowledge that he is the Lord?

Today's Walk with God

The greatest use of life is to spend it for something that will outlast it. - *William James*

Day 73

Christian Faith

"They replied, "Believe in the Lord Jesus, and you will be saved you and your household." - Acts 16:31 (NIV)

To have Faith in Christ means, trying to do all that God says. CS Lewis says, *"There would be no sense in saying you trusted a person if you would not take his advice."* Therefore, if you surrender yourself over to God, then this should be a demonstration that you are trying to obey Him.

Begin to build your Faith. Not by doing works or in the hope to get to Heaven. However, to turn to him and with this you will discover that the first gleam of Heaven is already inside you. He has begun to save you already.

Today's Walk with God

It is far better to live a holy life than to talk about it.
- DL Moody

Day 74

The Word only Works if you Work It & Walk It

"The law of the Lord is perfect, refreshing the soul. The statutes of the Lord are trustworthy making wise the simple. The precepts of the Lord are right, giving joy to the heart. The commands of the Lord are radiant, giving light to the eyes." - Psalm 19: 7-8 (NIV)

A recipe only works if you work it. The word of God is just like that. It has endured for more than 2700 years, yet every day you read it, you learn something new. On the other hand, if you leave it to gather dust, that's precisely what you'll get. It is the best recipe of life, like grandma's old recipes. Trying the recipe out may be daunting for others, you may have tried but failed, and never tried again. It may be like making a soufflé, will I rise or will I sink. Ask yourself what are the ingredients to making this work. Is my spirit in the right place? Do I actually want it to work for me? From whom are you seeking advice and interpretation of this recipe? Do you have the right equipment? Have you prepared yourself for the outcome? The only way the word of God works in our lives is that we need to work it and walk it. The benefits are great like the Psalmist says, it revives the soul, bring joy, it's trustworthy and radiant!

Today's Walk with God

Lord, today as I open my Bible and read your word, let me try implementing your recipes in my life. Let me begin to truly allow the word to work in my life, so that I may evermore walk with you. *Amen*

Day 75

I Cannot Fight in Saul's Armour

"Then Saul dressed David in his own tunic. He put a coat of armour on him and a bronze helmet on his head. 39 David fastened on his sword over the tunic and tried walking around, because he was not used to them. "I cannot go in these," he said to Saul, "because I am not used to them." So he took them off." - 1 Samuel 17:38-39 (NIV)

In Malcolm Gladwell's book, *David and Goliath: Underdogs, Misfits, and the Art of Battling Giants*, he shares a scientific, biological and pragmatic view on how David won that fight. How Goliath was visually impaired, and the armour he was carrying was never ready for David's attack.

We always say, don't fight fire with fire, and this is true in the strategy David used to win his battle. God gave us our unique fighting methods. When confronted with challenges, don't be tempted to copy another person's way.

Don't be intimidated by the opposition and the size of their weapons. You may feel feeble and small and attempt to do as they do; it will never work as effectively as your rock and sling. You can't beat me when I do what I do. Refuse to conform, follow the Holy Spirit, and he will guide you in your steps.

Today's Walk with God

Almighty Good, creator of all things. Thank you for the strength you have given me, the wisdom you have shown me as I put on my armour to fight my own Goliath. Bless me with the knowledge to discover my own armour today. In Jesus name, *Amen.*

Day 76

❧

From the Invisible to the Visible

"So we don't look at the troubles we can see now; rather, we fix our gaze on things that cannot be seen. For the things we see now will soon be gone, but the things we cannot see will last forever."
- 2 Corinthians 4: 18 (NLT)

Anything in life starts in the invisible and then become visible and possible. The secret sauce to the visible is what we call faith. For a moment close your eyes and imagine your future, your possibilities, the dreams and aspirations you have. Now, open your eyes and look at your current circumstance. You feel deflated, right? How can one reach their goals amidst their troubles? The word of God teaches us to never focus on our current status, but we need to gaze on the things we cannot see. It would be paramount if you made them so strong in your mind that the circumstance and situation bow down and surrenders to your dreams. Examine what kind of story are you telling yourself? Your story cannot justify your condition. You have the power to create your future, just like the women with the issue of blood her focus was so dominant on just touching Jesus's garment that when she did, he felt the power leave him, and at that moment she was healed. What are you looking at?

Today's Walk with God

Father, open my eyes, give me a different perspective to my story. Today, I choose to focus on what is ahead of me and the promised made for me. I refuse to be confined to today situations as they are temporary and will never last. Abide me Lord Jesus. *Amen*

Day 77

The Peace of God

"Let the peace of Christ rule in your hearts, since as members of one body you were called to peace. And be thankful."
- **Colossians 3:15 (NIV)**

If you ever wanted to know the voice of God know that Peace is the voice of God, it is the Holy Spirit.

The absence of peace is often plagued with doubt and anxiety, and this usually comes up when we are in disagreement or disobedience to the word of God, because we focus on the problem and not what God says about the issue. Even in Isaiah 48: 17-18, God says;

"I am the Lord your God, who teaches you what is best for you, who directs you in the way you should go. If only you had paid attention to my commands, your peace would have been like a river, your well-being like the waves of the sea."

Today's Walk with God

As we walk with God, Let the peace of God be your guide, your antenna, your true north, and then you will always be led back to the right path! *Amen*

Day 78

#No More Distraction

"He existed before anything else, and he holds all creation together."
- Colossians 1:17 (NIV)

In today's world of hashtags, I decided to start one of my own and called it **#nomoredistraction.** The purpose of this was to bring into focus, my life's purpose and meaning. I find that the world throws you all sort of distractions, some are very enticing and with great opportunity. It may be a new job, a business opportunity, an exciting projects your colleagues and friends what you to participate it. If you are not careful, you will be pulled in all sides, leaving you confused, ineffective, and depleted.

The book of Colossians reminds us where our focus should be, it says Jesus Christ existed before anything else, and he holds all creation together. The lesson is to learn to bring things into order. It is a sign of maturity, as you take in more, you always have to recalibrate and bring in a new order with Christ purpose and intention for your life.

What I discovered in the process of bringing things into focus is that everybody's vision for your life isn't always good for you, and if you don't have focus, you may be following other people's vision for your life and not yours.

Ask yourself today, what is your 'center,' define it, and focus on it and its principles. The distractions will take care of themselves. You will find yourself knowing what to say NO to quickly, as they are no longer part of your path.

The story about the pruning of branches is a great metaphor; there has to be cutting for growth to happen, and for you to bear fruit. Go and prune the areas in your life that are no longer serving you and God's plan for your life. You cannot climb the ladder of somebody else's thoughts.

Today's Walk with God

Dear God, I find myself being distracted and not having focus in life. Help me to discover my purpose, plan and the discipline to do what you have called me to accomplish. You are the vine in which I draw my strength. Show me what I need to prune in my life and the comfort that I am on the right path. I ask these in your name. *Amen.*

Day 79

Koinonia

*"We proclaim to you what we have seen and heard, so that you also may have fellowship with us. And our fellowship is with the Father and with his Son, Jesus Christ. We write this to make our joy complete." - **1 John 1:3-6 (NIV)***

One of the ministries I love to serve in is the Happening Ministry. Each year we host it at a Catholic Convent called *Koinonia*. I decided to find out what the word *koinonia* meant. According to Merriam-Webster dictionary, the word *koinonia* is a Greek word, it's meaning is around, the Christian fellowship or body of believers or intimate spiritual communion and participative sharing in a common religious commitment and spiritual community.

In the English language, we use it in the context of "fellowship," not from a companionship view but the communion with the Godhead of the Father and the Son and the Holy Spirit. It is, therefore, a participation of the human experience in communion with the living God himself. Paul, in his teachings, encouraged all of us to be in *koinonein* with each other and with God.

Today's Walk with God

Almighty Father, you call upon us to be in communion with you in our daily living. Help me to commune with you, to fellowship with you, to know you intimately so that my every day walk with you is guided by you. *Amen*

Day 80

～

The Last Supper and a New Mandate

The Thursday before Good Friday is often referred to as *'Maundy'* Thursday, it is derived from the Latin word *mandatum*, meaning commandment, it refers to the commands Jesus gave his disciples at the Last Supper: To love with humility by serving one another and to remember his sacrifice.

As we recall the scripture from *John 13: 1-5,* it read;

It was just before the Passover Festival. Jesus knew that the hour had come for him to leave this world and go to the Father. Having loved his own who were in the world, he loved them to the end. The evening meal was in progress, and the devil had already prompted Judas, the son of Simon Iscariot, to betray Jesus. Jesus knew that the Father had put all things under his power and that he had come from God and was returning to God; so he got up from the meal, took off his outer clothing, and wrapped a towel around his waist.
After that, he poured water into a basin and began to wash his disciples' feet, drying them with the towel that was wrapped around him.

John 13:12-17 His mandate to us;

When he had finished washing their feet, he put on his clothes and returned to his place. "Do you understand what I have done for you?" he asked them. "You call me 'Teacher' and 'Lord,' and rightly so, for that is what I am. Now that I, your Lord and Teacher, have washed your feet, you also should wash one another's feet. I have set you an example that you should do as I have done for you.

Very truly I tell you, no servant is greater than his master, nor is a messenger greater than the one who sent him. Now that you know these things, you will be blessed if you do them.

Today's Walk with God

There is no respect for others without humility in one's self. It was pride that changed angels into devils; it is humility that makes men as angels. Humility is not thinking less of yourself, it's thinking of yourself less. It is unwise to be too sure of one's own wisdom. *Amen*

My Prayer of Fellowship

WALK WITH HUMILITY

There is nothing noble in being superior to your fellow man; true nobility is being superior to your former self.
Ernest Hemingway

"No one can get Joy by merely asking for it. It is one of the ripest fruits of the Christian life, and, like all fruits, must be grown."

Henry Drummond

Day 81

At the Lord's Feet

"If my people, who are called by my name, will humble themselves and pray and seek my face and turn from their wicked ways, then I will hear from heaven, and I will forgive their sin and will heal their land." -2 Chronicles 7:14 (NIV)

Once upon a time, there was a man who was asked, "What did you gain by regularly praying to God?" The man replied, "Nothing... however, let me tell you what I did lose: anger, ego, greed, depression, insecurity, and fear of death."

The act of prayer is one of humble access. When you are at the Lord's feet, there no room for self-righteousness. Sometimes the answer to our prayers is not gaining but losing, which eventually is the gain.

Today's Walk with God

Almighty, we are not worthy, so much as to gather up the crumbs under your table. Teach us to be humble and lose our wicked way, so we may turn our faces towards you always. *Amen*

Day 82

Don't Judge a Book by its Cover

"My brothers and sisters, believers in our glorious Lord Jesus Christ must not show favouritism. Suppose a man comes into your meeting wearing a gold ring and fine clothes, and a poor man in filthy old clothes also comes in. If you show special attention to the man wearing fine clothes and say, "Here's a good seat for you," but say to the poor man, "You stand there" or "Sit on the floor by my feet," have you not discriminated among yourselves and become judges with evil thoughts?" - **James 2:1-4 (NIV)**

I was told a story once, about an Under Secretary of Defence in the United States, Mr. Simon Sinek, who gave a speech about how we are all Styrofoam cups. Styrofoam cups are those white non-biodegradable cups we all get at the office for coffee which always get thrown away. I thought that's what Simon may have thought of us. His story relates to the text in James. His speech went like this:

"*You know,* he said, interrupting his own speech, "*I spoke here last year. I presented at this same conference on this same stage. But last year, I was still an Under Secretary,*" he said." *I flew here in business class and when I landed, there was someone waiting for me at the airport to take me to my hotel. Upon arriving at my hotel,* he continued, *there was someone else waiting for me. They had already checked me into the hotel, so they handed me my key and escorted me up to my room. The next morning, when I came down, again there was someone waiting for me in the lobby to drive me to this same venue that we are in today.*

I was taken through a back entrance, shown to the greenroom and handed a cup of coffee in a beautiful ceramic cup. But this year, as I stand here to speak to you, I am no longer the Under Secretary, he continued.

I flew here coach class and when I arrived at the airport yesterday there was no one there to meet me. I took a taxi to the hotel, and when I got there, I checked myself in and went by myself to my room. This morning, I came down to the lobby and caught another taxi to come here. I came in the front door and found my way backstage. Once there, I asked one of the techs if there was any coffee. He pointed to a coffee machine on a table against the wall. So I walked over and poured myself a cup of coffee into this Styrofoam cup, he said as he raised the cup to show the audience. *It occurs to me, the ceramic cup they gave me last year . . . it was never meant for me at all. It was meant for the position I held. I deserve a Styrofoam cup."*

In the Bible text, James cautions us all about how we should treat one another, no matter what race, class, social standing we have. As believers, let us not judge one another. Like Simon Sinek, he was judged by his social standing, yet he was still the same man. Think about how you treat others who are different from you. Do they deserve to be Styrofoam cups?

Today's Walk with God

Lord Jesus, teach me to be humble, to recognise your creation. Forgive me for ever diminishing other and their value. Help me to remember that we are all equally and wonderfully made in your image. *Amen*

Day 83

What Fruit are You Producing?

*"But the fruit of the Spirit is love, joy, peace, patience, kindness, goodness, faithfulness, gentleness and self-control. Against such things there is no law." - **Galatians 5:22-23 (ESV)***

The Bible speaks about the fruit of the spirit. What is significant is the last line of the scripture. Against such, there is no law.

It indicates that these fruits come from the heart, they are not legislated, they cannot be regulated, and you will not stand in front of the court of man to be judged for them. Your judgement will come from God.

If we do not have these fruit of the spirit, what then are we producing? Is it jealousy, hatred, and anger?

Let us check what we nurture and grow in our spirit. If what you find is not pleasing, by God's grace and mercy, we are all forgiven and can, therefore, start anew. Go and bear the fruit of the Spirit like Christ.

Today's Walk with God

No one can get Joy by merely asking for it. It is one of the ripest fruits of the Christian life, and, like all fruits, must be grown. *Henry Drummond*

Day 84

A Woman Lesson to Her Son &
Now a Lesson for our Daughters

"The words of King Lemuel, the utterance which his mother taught him." - Proverbs 31: 1-10 (NJKV)

In this passage, we see King Lemuel reciting and probably teaching his subjects what his mother taught him. She most probably knew her son was next in line to be King, and so she took the time to teach him wisdom and the things of God.

Dear daughter of God, you may not know what lies within your children but take the time to be with them and to teach them Gods ways. Great rulers had mothers, so did evil rulers. Teach your children and train them in the way they should go.

Our children are blessings from God and must be raised, nurtured, and loved to become godly seeds for His kingdom. Never under-estimate the power and influence God has vested in mothers over their children's lives. Speak God's word over them. Show them the love and loving nature of God from a tender age. Let your children see how much God loves them through you.

Today's Walk with God

Giving birth and being born brings us into the essence of creation, where the human spirit is courageous and bold and the body, a miracle of wisdom. - *Harriette Hartigan*

Day 85

The Land of the Upright People

"For the grace of God has appeared that offers salvation to all people. It teaches us to say "No" to ungodliness and worldly passions, and to live self-controlled, upright and godly lives in this present age."
- Titus 2:11-12 (NIV)

There is a country in Africa that tried to live up to the words of this scripture, by naming it Burkina Faso. On 4 August 1984, the country's president Thomas Sankara decided to change the country's name to Burkina Faso from what was called the Upper Volta. He settled on two names after two main languages of the country: the Moore and the Dioula. *Burkina* from *Mòoré* means 'men of integrity,' while *Faso* in *Diouala* means 'fatherland.' Thus Burkina Faso is 'the land of upright people' or 'the land of honest people.'

This president was visionary and revolutionary in trying to improve the livelihood of his people. It was to be his mission to change his country. What a noble cause, indeed. The same call is made to all us, to refuse the ways of the world and say no to ungodliness, to live self-controlled and upright lives.

Become a *Burkinabé*, a person from the land of the upright.

Today's Walk with God

Jesus Christ, let me follow your way, cleanse me from my sin, so that I may be clean and upright in your sight. *Amen*

Day 86

Failure is the First Action In Learning

"Therefore, since we are surrounded by such a great cloud of witnesses, let us throw off everything that hinders and the sin that so easily entangles. And let us run with perseverance the race marked out for us, fixing our eyes on Jesus, the pioneer and perfecter of faith. For the joy set before him he endured the cross, scorning its shame, and sat down at the right hand of the throne of God. Consider him who endured such opposition from sinners, so that you will not grow weary and lose heart."
- Hebrews 12:1-3 (NIV)

I used to be afraid of failure so much that I became a workaholic. Nowadays, in the world of social media, FOMO (fear of missing out), in the world of Instagram and Twitter, you cannot share any of your failures. So much pressure today to present yourself perfectly. I came across this acronym about failure in the notes from one of the life coaching sessions I attended. It describes the word FAIL as, the First, Action, In, Learning. Our education system doesn't teach this. It shows us that failure is the end of it. Imagine if Thomas Edison gave up on his experiments? We would not have the light bulb. Imagine if the Wright brothers quit after their first attempt at making an airplane. Imagine if Jesus decided to quit, at the Garden of Gethesmane. Failure is the first action in learning. God teaches us to throw off everything that hinders us and the sin that entangles us. These are distractions, beliefs, and conditions that would make you want to quit. He is saying, fix your eyes on your Jesus, and you will reach your destination.

Today's Walk with God

Failure will never overtake me if my determination to succeed is strong enough. *Og Mandino*

Day 87

Seeking the Man Above Reproach

"Here is a trustworthy saying: Whoever aspires to be an overseer desires a noble task. Now the overseer is to be above reproach, faithful to his wife, temperate, self-controlled, respectable, hospitable, able to teach, not given to drunkenness, not violent but gentle, not quarrelsome, not a lover of money. He must manage his own family well and see that his children obey him, and he must do so in a manner worthy of full respect. (If anyone does not know how to manage his own family, how can he take care of God's church?)"
- 1 Timothy 3:1-5 (NIV)

We all know of the Proverb 31 woman. It has been drilled & recited by women across all churches, but the equivalent characteristics of the man, I have never really seen until the scripture in Timothy.

The scripture provides the character of a *good* man and also assigns characteristics of good leadership.

If you are looking for a good man, here are some of the cues to look out for. To find a good man is to be a good wife, cultivate your character, be the best you can be, and he who matches your character will follow.

Today's Walk with God

Lord God, teach me to cultivate the character that is above reproach in my walk with you, so that I too may be able to aspire to be a leader. *Amen*

Day 88

Trees Change their Leaves and not their Roots

"But examine everything carefully; hold fast to that which is good."
-1 Thessalonians 5:21 (NASB)

Human beings are like trees, with every season they change, they lose their leaves in winter, change their colours in autumn, regenerate new leaves in spring and bear fruit and flower in the summer.

We change our opinions, make different decisions daily, but one thing that should stay firm is our principles. It is how we are rooted. Examine your life today and figure out if your roots are deep enough to withstand the changing seasons of life. Ask yourself if you are easily swayed by the world and what is trending at the time. Have you sat down to determine what your values and principles are? It is crucial to stay firm in your principles; this is what will determine what kind of fruit you will bear.

Today's Walk with God

Hold on to what is good even if it is a handful of earth. Hold on to what you believe even if it is a tree which stands by itself. Hold on to what you must do even if it is a long way from here. Hold on to life even when it is easier letting go. Hold on to my hand even when I have gone away from you. Hold on to what is good. *Amen. Nancy Wood (1974)*

Day 89

Lock me in Lord

"Pairs of all creatures that have the breath of life in them came to Noah and entered the ark. The animals going in were male and female of every living thing, as God had commanded Noah. Then the Lord shut him in." & *"The waters flooded the earth for a hundred and fifty days."* **- Genesis 7:15-16 & 24 (NIV)**

As we prepare for the Happening Ministry, one of the days in preparation for the weekend is what we call a Lock-in, this is a time of spiritual instruction and commissioning before we go and minister to others. We devote the time in prayer and ask the Holy Spirit to guide us as we embark on the work of God's Kingdom. Noah did the same thing. As he was preparing for the great floods, he collected all of God's creatures for safekeeping into the Ark. Once they were all in. God shut them in.

He sealed them inside His Ark. You see, God always knows what is ahead of us and helps us to prepare for the future, which is unknown. He locks us in, gives us instruction, and we must be faithful and obedient to his direction. If Noah did not have faith, I don't believe he could have survived the 150 days in the Ark. It was God Himself who shut him in, to shut out the waters of the flood. God can shut out the dangers of this world from you; he can shut out diseases, pain, hurt in your life if we only surrender to his instruction. No matter how long it takes, he knows how to deal with your infirmities.

Today's Walk with God

May the Almighty God seal us inside His Ark of protection; give us patience and faith to weather the storms. *Amen*

Day 90

I'm Swallowed Up

*"The engulfing waters threatened me, the deep surrounded me; seaweed was wrapped around my head. To the roots of the mountains I sank down; the earth beneath barred me in forever. But you, Lord my God, brought my life up from the pit. "When my life was ebbing away, I remembered you, Lord, and my prayer rose to you, to your holy temple." - **Jonah 2: 5-7 (NIV)***

We all know the story of Jonah and the Whale. A Sunday school classic. Jonah was running away from executing the Lord's instruction to go and spread the Good News. While on a boat a rough storm hit their boat and he was blamed for the storm. The other sailors decided to throw him overboard. At that moment, God sent a large fish to swallow him up, and after three days, it spat him out. Jonah was swallowed up by life; it seemed he just wanted to hide and do nothing, to bury his head in the sand. We've all had *Jonah moments*, where we felt like we've just been thrown overboard, it is either you sink or swim. Most of us give up in despair and fall to the bottom of the ocean and hope to die. God shows us in this story that, even though you may forsake him and the world turns on you, He is still God Almighty, he will send the giant fish to swallow you up and rescue you from your misery and despair. No situation is temporary. In three days you will be on your way again.

Today's Walk with God

Lord Almighty, you are the God that can calm the raging seas, the one that gives mercy, the rescuer of our lives. Pull me out of my depression and despair. Restore hope and faith in my life. *Amen*

My Prayer of Humility

WALK INTO YOUR DESTINY

Destiny is not for comfort seekers.
Destiny is for the daring and
determined who are willing to endure
some discomfort, delay gratification,
and go where Destiny leads.
TD Jakes

"Carve your name on hearts, not tombstones. A legacy is etched into the minds of others and the stories they share about you."

Shannon L. Alder

Day 91

Understanding the Resurrection

"But if Christ is preached as raised from the dead, how can some among you say there is no resurrection of the dead? If there is no resurrection of the dead, then neither has Christ been raised....For if the dead are not raised, neither has Christ been raised."
- 1 Corinthians 15:12-19 (NABRE)

I grew and still worship in the Anglican Church and had recited the Nicene Creed, a declaration of our faith and part of it says, *"We look for the Resurrection the dead, and the life of the world come."*

It is another promise that God has promised us. Death is something we avoid thinking of, yet death, in the passing of our Lord Jesus Christ, is the one thing we celebrate the most, and it is because, in his death, there is life.

Today's Walk with God

We cannot pray in love & live in hate & still think we are worshipping God. - *A. W Tozer*

Day 92

But Jesus, Where are you Going?

"I have told you this, so that when their time comes you will remember that I warned you about them. I did not tell you this from the beginning because I was with you, but now I am going to him who sent me. None of you asks me, 'Where are you going?' Rather, you are filled with grief because I have said these things. But very truly I tell you, it is for your good that I am going away. Unless I go away, the Advocate will not come to you; but if I go, I will send him to you. When he comes, he will prove the world to be in the wrong about sin and righteousness and judgment: about sin, because people do not believe in me;"
- John 16:4-10 (NIV)

The disciples were in search of the answer to where Jesus might be going. They did not have the wisdom to interpret Jesus message. His ministry on earth was about to end, and he was going back to the Father who sent him. When we were young we clung to our parents especially on the first day of school, we did not want to let go, but we knew that we are going to be left in a safe and teaching environment. We did not want to grow and part from our parents! We did not know that when left behind, that's when we are truly going to begin our journey of learning.

Imagine if Jesus never left us? He knew exactly where he was going. Do you know where you are going?

Today's Walk with God

Lord Jesus, help me to walk on my own and in my own strength, Give me the vision to know where I'm going, because you will be there with me. *Amen*

Day 93

I Am the Salt of the Earth! I Am the Light of the World!

"You are the salt of the earth. But if the salt loses its saltiness, how can it be made salty again? It is no longer good for anything, except to be thrown out and trampled underfoot. "You are the light of the world. A town built on a hill cannot be hidden. Neither do people light a lamp and put it under a bowl. Instead they put it on its stand, and it gives light to everyone in the house. In the same way, let your light shine before others, that they may see your good deeds and glorify your Father in heaven".- Matthew 5:13-16 (NIV)

When God comes to give you good news! Don't be like Sarah, in *Genesis 18:9*. She hid behind the door. We often shy away from our shine, because we either think that we don't deserve it, or we doubt our capabilities. (Some call it the Imposter Syndrome)

In this passage, Matthew is trying to tell us that God made you special, unique, and talented, and if we do not exercise who we are, we lose our salt, our taste.

He further says that we should stand on mountain tops and let our light shine. Please share it with the world so that, as they see it, they may also spread theirs.

Today's Walk with God

Lord, I rest secure now and always, in the great knowledge that I belong to you and you will in no way abandon, reject or leave me. *Amen*

Day 94

Shackles

"As a prisoner for the Lord, then, I urge you to live a life worthy of the calling you have received." - Ephesians 4:1 (NIV)

"But to each one of us grace has been given as Christ apportioned it. This is why it[a] says: "When he ascended on high, he took many captives and gave gifts to his people." -Ephesians 4: 7-8 (NIV)

You and I spend our lifetime being prisoners of our dreams. We hold our destinies at ransom with self-created limitations, fear, religion, class, levels of education, race, image, etc... We put on the shackles on our feet and our wrists. They have become so comfortable that we are quick to use them when given an opportunity,

We chain ourselves to the couch; we chain ourselves to the bottle. We chain ourselves to self-pity...... *'Timothy Traddle, what are we going to do?'*

I say, thrust your life into a pool of passion for what you love, be like the pig and enjoy the mud, it may not look pretty for others, but to you, you know you are having the time of your life! Dive in with determination, for your dreams are the fuelling force of life.

Today's Walk with God

Shackle yourself with peace, love, with an unrelenting spirit. May your spirit be ignited today. *Amen*

Day 95

What Will We Boast About?

"Indeed, we felt that we had received the sentence of death. But that was to make us rely not on ourselves but on God who raises the dead". - 2 Corinthians 1:9 (NIV)

"For our boast is this, the testimony of our conscience, that we behaved in the world with simplicity and godly sincerity, not by earthly wisdom but by the grace of God, and supremely so toward you. For we are not writing to you anything other than what you read and understand and I hope you will fully understand just as you did partially understand us that on the day of our Lord Jesus you will boast of us as we will boast of you."
- 2 Corinthians 1:12-14 (NIV)

Paul was writing to the church of God at Corinth, with all the saints in the whole of Achaia and the question he asked was, *"What will we boast about in the second coming of Christ?"*

He writes to the church and makes it clear about how they would be remembered; it is about simplicity, sincerity, and attaining wisdom by the grace of God. He did not want the church to be remembered for its conquests, its works, it tithes, or how big their membership was? He is reminding us of the message of Jesus Christ, one of obedience, surrender, and servant-hood. These are the things we should hold in high regard! The flesh calls for us to boast about our accomplishment, yet we are called to be different.

Today's Walk with God

Carve your name on hearts, not tombstones. A legacy is etched into the minds of others and the stories they share about you.   *-Shannon L. Alder*

Day 96

Meeting "Mr Wrong" is part of the Master's Plan

"The woman said to him, "Sir, give me this water so that I won't get thirsty and have to keep coming here to draw water." He told her, "Go, call your husband and come back." "I have no husband," she replied. Jesus said to her, "You are right when you say you have no husband. The fact is, you have had five husbands, and the man you now have is not your husband. What you have just said is quite true." "Sir," the woman said, "I can see that you are a prophet."
"Woman, believe me, a time is coming when you will worship the Father neither on this mountain nor in Jerusalem. The woman said, "I know that Messiah" (called Christ) "is coming. When he comes, he will explain everything to us." Then Jesus declared, "I, the one speaking to you—I am he."- John 4: 15-18, 21, 25-26

She was part of the master plan – The Master's [Jesus] plan. It was no coincidence that they met and had this conversation, she was the key in fulfilling the mission of Jesus Christ, and yet her life's testimony of meeting Mr. Wrongs was the part of the deliverance of so many people. So do not be discouraged by your past; your story has power and healing power. Never be ashamed, be like this woman and go out into town and proclaim the Good News. How what seemed Wrong turned out to be so Right for so many people. You may be nameless, but your story has the power to free so many others.

Today's Walk with God

Lord Jesus, just like you shared the truth with the Samaritan woman; reveal my truth, so I too may be set free to glorify your name. *Amen*

Day 97

❧

Your Destiny is Not Tied to Anyone

*"If your right eye causes you to sin, tear it out and throw it away. For it is better that you lose one of your members than that your whole body be thrown into hell. And if your right hand causes you to sin, cut it off and throw it away. For it is better that you lose one of your members than that your whole body go into hell." - **Matthew 5: 29-30 (NIV)***

The courage of walking away is a demonstration of strength and dignity and the realisation that you are not betraying yourself or your values. We often stick around in dangerous situations, and while sticking around, we diminish our worth and value. We are like still waters that run deep, running deep with resentment, discontent, and frustration, hoping that something would make the river flow. In high school, my Geography teacher taught us about river structures, in particular about the oxbow lake. It is a lake formed after it has been cut off from the mainstream because of its meander.

You may have collected people around you that are oxbow lakes. They need to be cut off from your flow because they have become stagnant, and stagnation causes contamination. Your destiny is not tied to anyone. It is hard to follow someone when they are not moving. I have learned to say goodbye, and to know when that part of the story is over. God orders my steps.

Today's Walk with God

Lord you have ordered my steps. Show me the areas in my life I need to let go of, the people and things that no longer serve you. Teach me to say goodbye in humility and dignity, and to allow a refreshing of the spirit in my life. *Amen*

Day 98

The Bible, the Word of God

"Man does not live on bread alone, but on every work that comes from the mouth of God." - ***Matthew 4:4(NIV)***

Over and over again, we are encouraged to read our Bible daily, meditate on it, let it guide our steps, yet how many of us do so diligently? It is a real challenge in the busy-ness of our lives, and we forget to enquire, touch base on the word of God. Even in the advent of technology, how deeply do we engage with what is written? We have to learn to dig deeper and set aside the time to do so.

The bible is our constitution; it contains our rights and our privileges. I want to encourage you today to set aside 15min to read your Bible, to explore and question the text you have found and share it with the community around you.

Today's Walk with God

Heavenly Father, help me not to merely hear your word, but also to live according to it every day. Make me a doer of your word from today on. *Amen*

Day 99

His Attitude, My Attitude

Now when Jesus saw the crowds, he went up on a mountainside and sat down. His disciples came to him, and he began to teach them.
- Matthew 5:1-12 (NIV)

He said:
"Blessed are the poor in spirit,
for theirs is the kingdom of heaven.
Blessed are those who mourn,
for they will be comforted.
Blessed are the meek,
for they will inherit the earth.
Blessed are those who hunger and thirst for righteousness,
for they will be filled.
Blessed are the merciful,
for they will be shown mercy.
Blessed are the pure in heart,
for they will see God.
Blessed are the peacemakers,
for they will be called children of God.
Blessed are those who are persecuted because of righteousness,
for theirs is the kingdom of heaven.
"Blessed are you when people insult you, persecute you and falsely say all kinds of evil against you because of me. Rejoice and be glad, because great is your reward in heaven, for in the same way they persecuted the prophets who were before you.

Today's Walk with God

God is going to do something big in your life. Don't quit. Don't give up. Trust His timing. He is faithful and will complete what He started. *Amen*

Day 100

When Women Walk with God

*"Commit to the LORD whatever you do, and your plans will succeed." - **Proverbs 16:3 (NIV)***

I have learned that the Christian walk is a winding road. There will be times of joy, times of sorrow. God never leaves us or forsakes us. He has been with us each 365 days of the year. He will continue to do so.

We need to exercise commitment, which requires discipline, consistency, and hard work, if we allow ourselves to develop these skills inevitably, we will reach our destinations.

God will have seen our toil and labour and then bless you with the fruits of our work. When you put your plans before him, they will succeed.

Today's Walk with God

Help us Lord,
To live in your light
To act in your might
To think in your wisdom
To walk in your kingdom
To abide in your love
Your presence to prove
Amen
David Adam, Times and Seasons (Triangle, 1989)

When Women Walk with God
............they reach their destination

_____
_____
_____
_____
_____
_____
_____
_____
_____
_____
_____
_____
_____
_____
_____
_____
_____
_____
_____
_____
_____
_____
_____
_____
_____
_____
_____
_____
_____

If you have loved the devotional, please keep in touch us for more daily inspiration, devotion and prayer on our social media platforms.

Reference

Birch, J. (2010). *The Little Worship Leader's Helper*. Thanksgiving Press.

Doctor, T. S. (n.d.). *The Soul Doctor - Timeline Photos*. Retrieved from http://pinquity.net/the-soul-doctor-timeline/29414203793802779/

Graham, B. (n.d.). *http://www.goodreads.com/quotes/7237162-the-highest-form-of-worship-is-the-worship-of-unselfi*.

Halsall, R. (2017). *The Provincial President's New Year Message*. Mother's Union The Provincial President – West Indies.

Ignatian Prayer, J. H. (n.d.). *http://www.ignatianspirituality.com/12297/teach-me-to-be-generous*.

James, W. (1935). *The Thought and Character of William James: As Revealed in Unpublished Correspondence and Notes*.

Lodge, C. (2015, July 30). *10 inspirational quotes from William Wilberforce*. RetrievedfromCHRISTIANTODAY,https://www.christiantoday.com/article/10.inspirational.quotes.from.william.wilberforce/60570.htm

Manser, M. H. (n.d.). In *The Westminster Collection of Christian Quotations* (p. 116).

Marx, K. (1897). Letter from Marx To his Father. *The First writings of Karl Marx, (PDF) edited by Paul M. Schafer*.

Rice, H. S. (2010). A Collection Of Encouragement. Barbour Publishing Inc.

Sheldon, T. (n.d.). https://www.facebook.com/LikeTrentShelton/posts/427272910685348.

Sinek, S. (2016, June 24). *"We only deserve a styrofoam cup." – Simon Sinek*. Retrieved from https://bgallen.com/2016/06/24/we-only-deserve-a-styrofoam-cup-simon-sinek/

Spafford, H. (n.d.). *https://www.umcdiscipleship.org/resources/history-of-hymns-it-is-well-with-my-soul*.

Teresa, M. (n.d.). Retrieved from Christian Quotes: https://www.christianquotes.info/images/mother-teresa-quote-small-things-with-love/#axzz4gIf4hGhy

God loves you because He love you - YouTube. https://www.youtube.com/watch?v=NtX5zZMQHmE

About the Author

TJ Prince, (Tsholofelo Joy Prince) nee Tlhomelang is a writer, blogger, a publisher, entrepreneur, philanthropist and speaker, a member of community of believers in Sunninghill, Johannesburg, South Africa.

Her Facebook blog has over 20 000 readers, where she continues to share the word of God.

She is the owner of Huba Publishing Pty.Ltd. and founder of IgniteXperience a youth development programme aimed to teach the youth, self awareness and their identity in Christ. She is passionate about holistic women development, as she manages a women advancement programme in her organisation.

Her career spans in areas of social entrepreneurship, organisational behaviour, coaching & mentoring, leadership development and strategic planning.

www.ingramcontent.com/pod-product-compliance
Lightning Source LLC
Chambersburg PA
CBHW020501030426
42337CB00011B/192